D1737126

SUR PLUSIEURS
BEAUX
SUJECTS

SUR PLUSIEURS BEAUX SUJECTS

Wallace Stevens' Commonplace Book

A Facsimile and Transcription

Edited and Introduced by

Milton J. Bates

Stanford University Press
Stanford, California

Huntington Library
San Marino, California

© 1989 by the Henry E. Huntington Library
and Art Gallery

Printed in the United States of America
CIP data appear at the end of the book

for my parents

CONTENTS

ACKNOWLEDGMENTS

THIS PROJECT WAS VERY MUCH A COLLABORATION, and I am pleased to acknowledge those who helped me to complete it. George S. Lensing first proposed the edition; he, A. Walton Litz, and Glen MacLeod also read the manuscript and suggested several improvements. Timothy Gallagher helped me track many an entry to its published source, while Gene H. Bell-Villada, Wu-chi Liu, William F. McNaughton, Fan Shen, Holly Stevens, Joseph Wiesenfarth, and Alex Zwerdling supplied information on particular entries. To the staff of the Interlibrary Loan Office at the Marquette University Library, and especially to Patricia Bohach, I am grateful for securing items not available locally. Brigitte Coste and Steven Taylor amended my translations from the French, and Gregory Carlson, S.J., did the same for the Latin; mine, however, is the fault for any remaining errors or infelicities.

The Henry E. Huntington Library, besides permitting me to edit *Sur Plusieurs Beaux Sujects* and quote from manuscript materials in the Wallace Stevens Collection, served as an exemplary co-publisher; special credit belongs to the former director, Robert Middlekauff, and my editor, Guilland Sutherland. I am likewise grateful to Holly Stevens and the following institutions for permission to use unpublished items: the Department of Special Collections, University of Chicago Library; the Dartmouth College Library; Special Collections and Rare Books, Library of the University of Massachusetts at Amherst; and the Princeton University Library. Holly Stevens and Alfred A. Knopf, Inc. granted me permission to quote from the copyrighted works by Wallace Stevens. I am grateful, finally, to the American Council of Learned Societies, the Huntington Library, and Marquette University for financial assistance during crucial phases of my research.

INTRODUCTION

[Q]uotations have a special interest, since one
is not apt to quote what is not one's own
words, whoever may have written them. The
"whoever" is the quoter in another guise, in
another age, under other circumstances.
                                    — *Wallace Stevens*[1]

I

W. H. AUDEN MAINTAINED that biographies and autobiographies of writers are "always superfluous and usually in bad taste" because the writer is a maker rather than a man of action. Auden nevertheless acknowledged that his commonplace book could be read as "a sort of autobiography," as a transcript of his private world.[2] That world is *invented* in both senses of the word, being composed partly of makings, partly of findings. Wallace Stevens' commonplace book, likewise a repository of things made up and things come upon, might be read in much the same spirit. In the two slender notebooks which constitute *Sur Plusieurs Beaux Sujets*, he pursues the same examination of his life, ideas, and art that he pursues in his poems, lectures, and letters. Entries regarding the hero, the social role of the writer, the nature of modernism, and the influence of the past appear just about where one would expect to find them between 1932 and 1953; entries regarding imagination and reality are pervasive.

Whereas Auden's commonplace book reflects a mind that nourished itself on the richest and most provocative literature of all periods, including his

---

[1] Letter to Elsie Viola Kachel, 7 Jan. 1909. This unpublished letter is at the Huntington Library. I cite Stevens' published works parenthetically in my text and notes, using the conventional abbreviations for *The Collected Poems of Wallace Stevens* (*CP*, published in 1955); the *Opus Posthumous* (*OP*, 1957), ed. Samuel French Morse; *The Necessary Angel: Essays on Reality and the Imagination* (*NA*, 1951); the *Letters of Wallace Stevens* (*L*, 1966), *The Palm at the End of the Mind* (*PEM*, 1971), and *Souvenirs and Prophecies: The Young Wallace Stevens* (*SP*, 1977), ed. Holly Stevens. I quote from these copyrighted works with the permission of Holly Stevens and the publisher, Alfred A. Knopf, Inc.

Dates assigned to poems and essays indicate year of first publication; those to lectures, year of delivery; those to plays, year of first performance.

[2] *A Certain World: A Commonplace Book* (New York: Viking, 1970), p. vii.

1

own, Stevens' reflects a mind that drew sustenance from such unlikely materials as an entry in a rare book catalogue and an uplifting sentiment on the entablature of a building. He read creatively, in the manner recommended by Emerson, and acquired knowledge unsystematically, in the way Frost once compared to picking up burrs while walking in the fields. He ranged widely, it is true, over the periodical literature of his day, favoring the London *New Statesman and Nation* and French newspapers and magazines like *Le Figaro*, *Je Suis Partout*, *Labyrinthe*, *Marianne* (which regularly featured a column by Ramon Fernandez[3]), *La Nouvelle Revue Française*, *Le Point*, and *Le Temps*. But major works of modern literature are conspicuously absent from his commonplace book and rarer in his library than one would expect, given his interest in poetic theory.[4] To attribute this to the casual nature of his reading after a long day at the office is only to beg the question, for he had set himself a more ambitious intellectual course as a young lawyer in New York, before launching his poetic career.

Why, one wonders, would a major poet deny himself the stimulation of reading his contemporaries precisely during his most creative years? The reason is perhaps to be found in the commonplace book itself, specifically in an excerpt from a review of William Robinson's *The English Flower Garden*. Since Robinson's book was then in its fifteenth edition, the reviewer felt no obligation to assess its practical advice on seed and soil, weeding and mulching. Instead, linking the gardener's pastime to a broader category of human experience, he speculates, "The art of play, as also, I am inclined to think, the art of life itself, consists mainly in the creation of an environment within which we are of some importance" (Entry 7 in the text that follows). *Sur Plusieurs Beaux Sujects* was that kind of environment for Stevens, a plot to be cultivated and jealously guarded against intrusion by any idiom or idea he could not appropriate wholly for his own purposes. The commonplace book was in this respect an emblem of his imagination, whose integrity he likewise protected by not reading "highly mannered" poets like Eliot and Pound or studying "full-sized" philosophers like Plato and Aristotle (*L* 813, 476; cf. *L* 575).

This resourceful notebook was also an important resource for Stevens. Of the one hundred and four entries, he quoted or paraphrased twenty-two in his poems, lectures, essays, and letters—and this does not include the many

[3] Fernandez wrote a regular book review column for *Marianne*. Stevens acknowledged reading some of his criticism but protested that the Ramon Fernandez of "The Idea of Order at Key West" (1934) "was not intended to be anyone at all" (*L* 798).

[4] For more information about Stevens' library, see 1) the book auction catalogues published by Parke-Bernet Galleries of New York for sales numbers 1885 (10 Mar. 1959) and 1895 (7-8 Apr. 1959); 2) Peter Brazeau's "Wallace Stevens at the University of Massachusetts: Checklist of an Archive," *Wallace Stevens Journal*, 2 (Spring 1978), 51-52; and 3) my own "Stevens' Books at the Huntington: An Annotated Checklist," *Wallace Stevens Journal*, 2 (Fall 1978), 45-61; 3 (Spring 1979), 15-33; 3 (Fall 1979), 70. These provide an incomplete picture of Stevens' library, since after his death his widow sold many of his books to a bookseller who kept no record of the titles purchased.

entries whose themes he echoed without referring to them explicitly. If, as he once remarked, his lectures were "a kind of compost pile" for the poetry (*L* 627), then his commonplace book provided compost for all of his other writing, including the lectures. Several days before he read "Imagination as Value" at Yale in September 1948, he told a correspondent that he had done no reading for the paper (*L* 613-14). Yet the lecture is replete with quotations from Pascal, Cassirer, Pater, A. J. Ayer, C. E. M. Joad, Freud, Joyce, Gide, Vasari, Santayana, and Jean Paulhan. Some of these he found in books in his library.[5] For the material from Pascal, Joad, and Santayana, he was able to draw upon recent entries in *Sur Plusieurs Beaux Sujects* (see Entries 90-92). His commonplace book was apparently never far from hand or mind, for he sometimes used an entry years after excerpting it (see Entries 17, 18, 54, 67, 68).

II

SUR PLUSIEURS BEAUX SUJECTS opens with an excerpt from a 1932 issue of *Je Suis Partout*. Only by convention might this be called the beginning of his commonplace book, however, since it merely resumes a kind of thinking and writing he had been doing since at least his third semester at Harvard College. During that fall of 1898, he inaugurated his journal (reproduced in Holly Stevens' *Souvenirs and Prophecies*) with several excerpts from *The Life and Letters of Benjamin Jowett*, to which he added his own reflections.[6] These set the pattern for many of his journal entries over the next decade and, years later, for the commonplace book. Among the journal entries that would not seem out of place in *Sur Plusieurs Beaux Sujects* is the following, dated April 30 [1907]:

> *The Nation* No. 7 (London) p. 255[7]
>   "We must leave it to the aesthetic critics to explain why that is— why it is easier for nearly everyone to recognize the meaning of common reality after it has passed through another's brain—why thousands of kindly people should have contemplated negro slavery day by day for years without emotion, and then have gone mad over "Uncle Tom's Cabin.""

[5] Stevens' copy of Cassirer's *An Essay on Man* (quoted in *NA* 136) is at the Huntington Library, his copy of Freud's *The Future of an Illusion* (quoted in *NA* 139) at the University of Massachusetts Library.

[6] Evelyn Abbott and Lewis Campbell, *The Life and Letters of Benjamin Jowett, M. A., Master of Balliol College, Oxford*, 2 vols. (London: John Murray, 1897). Stevens' excerpts, in the order of their appearance in his journal (*SP* 19-20), are from II:78, I:165, and II:153; several pages have been removed from the journal between the first and second excerpts.

[7] "Propaganda by the Play," rev. of *Votes for Women*, by Elizabeth Robins, *Nation*, 13 Apr. 1907, p. 255; *recognize* is spelled *recognise* in the source. The *Nation* eventually became the *New Statesman and Nation*, from which Stevens took sixteen of the entries in *Sur Plusieurs Beaux Sujects*.

It is because common reality is being exhibited. It is being treated objectively.[8]

Like the best of the entries in *Sur Plusieurs Beaux Sujects*, this consists of an excerpt and citation plus Stevens' gloss—a gloss which suggests how his reading nourished his lifelong thematic preoccupations. In late poems like "The Plain Sense of Things" (1952), "Not Ideas about the Thing but the Thing Itself" (1954), and "Of Mere Being" (written about 1955) we find him still pondering the difference between common reality and that same reality "on exhibit" in literature or art.

Except for two entries written in the weeks immediately preceding his mother's death in 1912, the journal concludes on 14 May 1909 with eleven pages of notes, many of them culled from his reading at the Astor Library (*SP* 219-23). Several of these are in French or Latin, like some in *Sur Plusieurs Beaux Sujects*. Also anticipating his practice in the commonplace book, Stevens would draw upon these entries in subsequent writings. His attempt to capture the effect of two Oriental prints[9] in his journal—

> Pale orange, green and crimson, and white,
> and gold and brown
> Deep lapis-lazuli and orange, and opaque green, fawn-color,
> black and gold—

became an early manuscript poem entitled "Colors":

> – I –
> Pale orange, green and crimson, and
> White, and gold and brown.
>
> – II –
> Lapis-lazuli and orange, and opaque green,
> faun-color, black and gold.[10]

Another of the excerpts, a couplet from Browning's *Rabbi Ben Ezra*, would not surface until forty-six years later, in Stevens' speech accepting the National Book Award for his *Collected Poems*: "Now, at seventy-five, as I look back on the little that I have done and as I turn the pages of my own poems

---

[8] This entry is reproduced as it appears in the manuscript notebook at the Huntington Library; cf. *SP* 179.

[9] Here Stevens identifies these as "Japanese color prints" (*SP* 222). In a letter to Elsie of 18 Mar. 1909, he added a third "word painting" and described them as "all from the Chinese" (*L* 137).

[10] Reproduced in Robert Buttel, *Wallace Stevens: The Making of* Harmonium (Princeton: Princeton Univ. Press, 1967), p. 70. Stevens later parodied this kind of color impressionism in *Bowl, Cat and Broomstick* (1917, *PEM* 31).

gathered together in a single volume, I have no choice except to paraphrase the old verse that says that it is not what I am, but what I aspired to be that comforts me" (*OP* 246; cf. *SP* 220).

In 1904 Stevens met his future wife, Elsie Viola Kachel, and initiated a correspondence that would continue until their marriage in 1909. As he put more of himself into his letters, he put proportionally less into his journal. "My letters to Elsie," he wrote in his journal on 4 January 1907, "usurp the chronicles that, but for them, I should set down here" (*SP* 171). The letters usurped not only his "chronicles" but also the kind of material he later committed to his commonplace book. On 7 March 1909 he apprised Elsie of his method of gleaning material from his reading: "I make notes as I read on little slips of paper which, it is true, I throw away before long, but which are interesting for a while. —For instance, last night I saw something about 'March wind-mills' and promptly jotted it down. . . ."[11] Eleven days later, he sent Elsie several selections from the same "batch of notes" that eventually became part of his journal (*L* 137-38; cf. *SP* 222). Again in a letter of 9 May, after lamenting his neglect of the journal, he went on to say, "I wish I could put into it, without too much trouble, even a small part of the notes I have made at the Library. Let me preserve one by putting it in our Annals. . ." (*L* 142). Unable to stop with this tidbit, some verse by Laurence Binyon, he added further selections from his reading.

Stevens' journal and letters to Elsie are the more obvious antecedents of his commonplace book; less obvious are the marginalia in his books and some of the early poems responding to a published source. As a college student, he did not hesitate to use the margins of his books to define his own aesthetic convictions against those of Matthew Arnold, James Russell Lowell, and Walter Pater.[12] Later, he apparently developed scruples about "disfiguring" his books and restricted himself for the most part to page numbers and catch phrases on the dust jacket or back paste-down. Exceptions to this practice, besides his extensive marginal paraphrases in Charles Mauron's *Aesthetics and Psychology*, appear in his copies of Marianne Moore's *Selected Poems*, C. Day-Lewis' *The Magnetic Mountain*, Ferruccio Busoni's *Letters to His Wife*, and Nicolas Berdyaev's *Solitude and Society*, whose flyleaves bear pertinent excerpts from his reading in A. E. Powell's *The Romantic Theory of Poetry*, the *New Statesman and Nation*, *Hound and Horn*, the *London Mercury*, and *Philosophy*.[13]

Among Stevens' first mature poems are several—"Phases" (1914), "Lettres d'un Soldat" (1918), "Nuances of a Theme by Williams" (1918), and "Peter Parasol" (1919)—that take their departure from another text, usually in

---

[11] Letter at the Huntington Library.

[12] As a college student, Stevens owned and annotated Arnold's *Essays in Criticism* and *Essays in Criticism: Second Series*, the *Letters of James Russell Lowell* edited by Charles Eliot Norton, and Pater's *Appreciations, with an Essay on Style*. All are at the Huntington Library.

[13] Stevens' copy of *Solitude and Society* is at the University of Massachusetts Library; his copies of the books by Moore, Day-Lewis, and Busoni are at the Huntington Library.

French. Sometimes, as in Section IV of "Lettres d'un Soldat," Stevens' poem appears to be little more than a brief annotation of his text:

> *31 octobre*
> *Jusqu'à présent j'ai possedé une sagesse de*
> *renoncement, mais maintenant je veux une sagesse qui*
> *accepte tout, en s'orientant vers l'action future.*[14]
>
> MORALE
>
> And so France feels. A menace that impends,
> Too long, is like a bayonet that bends.
>
> (*OP* 13)

In this poem, as in his response to the discussion of *Uncle Tom's Cabin* quoted above, Stevens finds in another writer's specific, local observation a larger significance: what Eugène Lemercier feels personally during the prolonged stress of World War I is also what his country feels—indeed, what anyone would feel in a time of impending menace.

From one point of view, Lemercier's comment appears dwarfed by Stevens' "morale"; but it is not therefore unimportant, for the poem owes its very life to the tension between the individual and the universal, between the peculiar and the general. Pondering this phenomenon during the next world war, Stevens would conclude that the poet

> tries by a peculiar speech to speak
>
> The peculiar potency of the general,
> To compound the imagination's Latin with
> The lingua franca et jocundissima.
>
> ("Notes toward a Supreme Fiction," *CP* 397)

A significant element in the finished poem, Lemercier's sentence was crucial to its genesis. Like the other pieces mentioned above, "Lettres d'un Soldat" belongs to the period when Stevens was finding his poetic voice and seemed to require a lingua franca (if not always jocundissima) to quicken his imagination's Latin.

It is probably no coincidence that *Sur Plusieurs Beaux Sujects* opens in the early thirties, when Stevens was just beginning to rouse from the lethargy that had claimed his imagination after *Harmonium* (1923). No fewer than twenty-one entries date from 1934-1935, when he was also writing the poems of *Ideas of Order* (1935, 1936). Though his poetic activity during a given period does not always correspond to the number of entries in his commonplace book (if it did, there would be more than five entries for the highly productive

---

[14] *possedé*: sic, for *possédé*. "Until the present, I have possessed a wisdom of renunciation; but now I want a wisdom that accepts everything by directing itself toward future action."

years 1940-1942), one nevertheless suspects that the creative and annotative phases of his imagination were intimately related, especially when the poetry had to be coaxed into being.

Even during his more spontaneous epochs, Stevens' method of writing poetry resembled his method of gathering material for the commonplace book. A poem often came to him first as a title, which he jotted down on a scrap of paper; one of his notebooks, appropriately entitled *From Pieces of Paper*, contains the ungerminated seeds of many such poems.[15] That one French quotation appears in both *Sur Plusieurs Beaux Sujects* (as Entry 58) and *From Pieces of Paper* underscores the affinity between his annotative and creative phases. Some of the titles he actually developed, like "Anatomy of Monotony" (originally "Footnote To The Anatomy of Monotony") and "Celle Qui Fût Héaulmiette," were already "textualized" as titles before he took them up.[16] Others, such as "A High-Toned Old Christian Woman" and "Like Decorations in a Nigger Cemetery," were memorable if somewhat malicious phrases picked up in conversation with a friend.[17] Once in place, they served Stevens as texts to be glossed poetically, in much the same way he comments on excerpts from his reading. During composition, the poem itself passed through a "pieces of paper" stage before arriving at the final copy he gave to his typist (see *L* 316, 641).

Stevens' practice, then, tended to blur the distinction between texts he encountered in his reading and those he wrote himself; he responded intellectually and aesthetically to his own titles and *aperçus* as though they were suggestive passages in books or colorful phrases heard in passing. One sees a similar continuity between the entries in *Sur Plusieurs Beaux Sujects* and those in another pair of notebooks he began to keep in the early thirties, *Adagia* I and II. These are devoted for the most part to original aphorisms, some of which he published in 1940 and 1942.[18] As though to confound the tidy discriminations of his future editors, however, Stevens included among the *Adagia* a couple of entries that might just as well have appeared in *Sur Plusieurs Beaux Sujects*:

Goethe's *General-beichte* was written of another who "spake

---

[15] *From Pieces of Paper* and an earlier notebook entitled *Schemata*, also a source of Stevens' titles, are reproduced and discussed in George S. Lensing, *Wallace Stevens: A Poet's Growth* (Baton Rouge: Louisiana State Univ. Press, 1986), pp. 158-200.

[16] The title "Footnote To The Anatomy of Monotony" appears on a holograph draft of the poem at the Huntington Library. Stevens told Bernard Heringman in a letter of 21 July 1953 (copy at the Huntington) that "Celle Qui Fût Héaulmiette" was suggested by Rodin's sculpture *Celle qui fut la belle heaulmière*; Rodin, in turn, named his sculpture after the old courtesan in Villon's poem *Le Grand Testament*, one line of which reads, "La belle qui fut heaulmière . . ." (XLVII.2).

[17] Judge Arthur Powell of Atlanta provided Stevens with both of these titles. The poem "No Possum, No Sop, No Taters" and some of his letters to Elsie (see, for example, *L* 208, 233) also testify to Stevens' fascination with Southern speech.

[18] Thirty-nine aphorisms appeared under the title "Materia Poetica" in *View*, 1 (Sept. 1940), 3; and *View*, 2nd series, No. 3 (Oct. 1942), 28.

three thousand proverbs, and his songs were a thousand and five.
From Goethe proverbs poured incessantly."

Goethe: Felkin O Univ P. 1932.[19]

Usage is everything (*"Les idées sont destinées à être deformées à l'usage. Reconnâitre ce fait est une preuve de désinteressement."* Georges Braque. *Verve* No. 2).[20]

(*OP* 159)

Conversely, Stevens included in *Sur Plusieurs Beaux Sujects* a number of original aphorisms, like "Success as the result of industry is a peasant ideal" and "Success is to be happy with the wise" (Entries 3, 4). Or are these original? Certainly the wording is Stevens' own, and two previous editors of his *Adagia* have fittingly included them in that notebook. Yet these immediately follow two excerpts from Stevens' reading which are also on the subject of success. If not actually glosses, his aphorisms may have been suggested by the quoted texts.

Indeed, the distinction between quoting himself and quoting another writer of like mind might have seemed arbitrary to Stevens, given his conviction that "one is not apt to quote what is not one's own words, whoever may have written them." Moreover, the poet who wrote that "Poetry and materia poetica are interchangeable terms" (*OP* 159) would probably not have insisted on the generic distinction between original adage and gloss, between gloss and poem. Surveying the whole body of Stevens' writings—poems, lectures, essays, plays, journal, letters, aphorisms, marginalia, miscellaneous notebooks, commonplace book—one senses their underlying similarity. They share not only a kindred technique—slips of paper chafing the mind into making its pearl—but also a kindred way of thinking. We might take a moment, here, to examine that way of thinking, especially as disclosed in *Sur Plusieurs Beaux Sujects*.

III

IN HER SUGGESTIVE STUDY OF THE WAYS Stevens uses aphorism in his poetry, Beverly Coyle distinguishes between the "centripetal" and "centrifugal" tendencies in his thinking.[21] On the one hand, he used aphoristic statement to convey a sense of finality and closure; it satisfied his craving, as he once put it, "to seize an impression and lock it up in words" (*SP* 48). On the

[19] A. Walton Litz restores this entry, omitted from the *Opus Posthumous* collection of adages, in "Particles of Order: The Unpublished *Adagia*," in *Wallace Stevens: A Celebration* (Princeton: Princeton Univ. Press, 1980), p. 67.

[20] Properly accented, the French words should read *déformées, Reconnaître*, and *désintéressement*.

[21] *A Thought to be Rehearsed: Aphorism in Wallace Stevens's Poetry* (Ann Arbor: UMI Research Press, 1983).

other hand, he could not remain content with his own formulations; he was impelled to devise other, often contradictory pronouncements having the same air of authority and finality. In April 1906 he confided to his journal, "my opinions generally change even while I am in the act of expressing them. So it seems to me and so, perhaps, everyone thinks of himself. The words for an idea too often dissolve it and leave a strange one" (*SP* 165). Pursuing this thought later the same month, he wrote, "When you first feel the truth of, say, an epigram, you feel like making it a rule of conduct. But this one is displaced by that, and thus things go on in their accustomed way" (*SP* 166).

That this was a temperamental reflex and not merely the vacillation of youth is suggested by a letter written forty-three years later, wherein the seventy-year-old Stevens says, ". . . I don't really think that one's offhand remarks should be taken seriously. Some people always know exactly what they think. I am afraid that I am not one of those people. The same thing keeps active in my mind and rarely becomes fixed" (*L* 641). Is the poet irresponsible if he represents a world any less stable or monolithic than Dante's? A certain kind of reader will have it so, and will consider the apologetic tone of this letter to be entirely warranted. But the sympathetic reader will apply to Stevens what Graham Bell says of another artist in Entry 40 of the commonplace book: "With Cézanne integrity was the thing, and integrity never allowed him to become fixed at any one point in his development, but sent him onward toward new discoveries of technique, new realisations of the motive."

The dogmatic tone and definitive rhetorical form of Stevens' aphoristic statements belie, then, their speculative function. Like Henry James, whom he quotes in Entries 68 and 73, he had a mind so fine that no idea—certainly no single, fixed idea—could violate it.[22] Any given idea was but an assay of bias, a local indirection by which to find cosmic directions out. Hence what Stevens demanded of his supreme fiction, that it must change, he also demanded of his own thought. This is illustrated by an episode that took place in the fall of 1951, when he traveled to the University of Chicago to lecture on the poetry of certain philosophical ideas. At a dinner party prior to the lecture he met Elder Olson, who, not being privy to Stevens' intended topic, denied that ideas can be inherently poetic. In retrospect the younger poet was surprised at Stevens' willingness to entertain the antithesis of his own proposition. "He didn't argue," Olson recalled.

> He meditated. He struck me all the way through as a very reflective
> and reticent man. He would hear something, and you could see
> him think about it; you could practically hear him think about it.
> He spoke in sentences, not in paragraphs. There was no such thing

[22] These are of course Eliot's words in appreciation of James. Stevens marked only one passage in his copy of Randall Jarrell's *Pictures from an Institution* (New York: Knopf, 1954), now at the Huntington Library; it reads, "it is better to entertain an idea than to take it home to live with you for the rest of your life" (p. 173).

as a connected argument. What you had instead was a series of intuitive and highly perceptive remarks. When he got on a subject, he would talk with flashes of intuition. That was not a man who thought consecutively. You will find that to be the case with his essays from *The Necessary Angel* and *Opus Posthumous*. His real style was the "Adagia," and that was very much his conversational way.[23]

One *can* practically hear Stevens thinking aloud in the *Adagia*, where one aphorism is apt to be canceled by another in the vagaries of meditation. Sometimes, in fact, he qualifies himself crucially within the same adage:

> Literature is the better part of life. To this it seems inevitably necessary to add, provided life is the better part of literature.
>
> (*OP* 158)

> I have no life except in poetry. No doubt that would be true if my whole life was free for poetry.
>
> (*OP* 175)

Stevens' poetry is equally untroubled by the hobgoblin of consistency. There one sees the same pattern of self-contradiction and self-qualification—not only in that "endlessly elaborating poem," his poetic *oeuvre*, but also in the poetic sequences which were his congenial medium from "Carnet de Voyage" (1914) through "An Ordinary Evening in New Haven" (1949). "Contrary Theses," the title of two poems published in tandem in 1942, could have served as the title of other unlikely pairings. The romantic "Tea at the Palaz of Hoon," for example, follows hard upon the heels of the naturalistic "The Snow Man" in the October 1921 issue of *Poetry* magazine. Even in a single poem like "Chocorua to Its Neighbor" Stevens artfully plays contradictory statements against one another.[24]

As in the adages and poems, so in *Sur Plusieurs Beaux Sujects*: the centripetal effect of individual entries is offset by the centrifugal effect of the whole. This might be demonstrated by looking at three of the topics frequently addressed in the commonplace book—reality, the social role of the poet, and religious belief.

Except in cases where Stevens explicitly agrees or disagrees with the sentiment in an excerpt, one cannot know for sure how closely it corresponds to his own opinion. Judging from comments he makes elsewhere, however, one can infer that he accepts the view that significant art expresses the normal (Entry 9), that everyday things are as important as Scripture (Entry 23), that

---

[23] Quoted in Peter Brazeau, *Parts of a World: Wallace Stevens Remembered* (New York: Random House, 1983), p. 211.

[24] I consider this aspect of "Chocorua" in *Wallace Stevens: A Mythology of Self* (Berkeley: Univ. of California Press, 1985), pp. 246-47.

the artist who departs from common experience may end in futility (Entry 78), that poetry has as one of its most valuable functions the illumination of the usual (Entry 97). Yet Stevens also appears to endorse Henry James's proposition that it is art which "*makes* life, makes interest, makes importance" (Entry 68). "Poetry," he contends in one of the original aphorisms, "creates a fictitious existence on an exquisite plane" (Entry 37), and a couple of the excerpts echo the idea that reality is tedious and incoherent, something to be transcended or transformed rather than illuminated (Entries 101, 102).

Stevens managed to remain aloof from the social and political realities of the thirties until the Alcestis Press published his *Ideas of Order* (1935), which elicited Stanley Burnshaw's provocative review.[25] The same summer *Ideas of Order* appeared, *Sur Plusieurs Beaux Sujets* registered Stevens' awareness of the two social postures available to him were he to abandon what Burnshaw and other leftist writers called the "middle ground." Though Bertrand Russell is speaking of the philosopher in Entry 27, where he says that one can either concern oneself with public affairs or retire to a mountain-top and meditate, he could just as well be speaking of the writer. In subsequent entries, E. M. Forster discusses the writer's call to "rally humanity in the presence of catastrophe" (Entry 28), Jacques Maritain asserts that the artist can reshape the intellect of his time (Entry 47), and Nicola Chiaromonte ascribes the radical crisis in Italian society to liberal intellectuals who lacked genuine feeling for their fellow men (Entry 69). But for every entry that suggests acceptance of a social role, there is another warning of the dangers of vulgarization (Entries 81, 95) or extolling the courageous self-reliance of the artist who goes his own way, regardless of the demands of society (Entries 31, 64, 76).

The poet who wrote "A High-Toned Old Christian Woman" (1922) and other poems that seek to *épater le croyant* is also at work in the commonplace book. He exalts "genteel exercises" over the fear of God by recommending deletion of a phrase in Entry 11, shares a reviewer's wry amusement at Victorian eschatology (Entry 59), and looks to poetry rather than Jesus for salvation (Entry 82). At the same time, however, he speculates that the pleasure of poetry may derive from divine beauty (Entry 21), invokes the idea of divine election to account for the poet's gift (Entry 71), takes note of Jehovah's covenant with Noah as recorded in the Book of Genesis (Entry 72), and entertains André Rousseaux's notion that philosophical works, novels, and poems all spring from a nostalgia for the eternal if not from a belief in immortality (Entry 83).

The contradictions that beset these entries on reality, social concern, and religion will surprise no one who is familiar with Stevens' published works. Their eclectic, centrifugal character is more obvious in *Sur Plusieurs Beaux Sujets* because these fragments have been snatched from such a variety of languages, authors, and historical periods. The discontinuity of lexical surface

---

[25] "Turmoil in the Middle Ground," *New Masses*, 1 Oct. 1935, pp. 41-42; reprinted in *Wallace Stevens: The Critical Heritage*, ed. Charles Doyle (London: Routledge and Kegan Paul, 1985), pp. 137-40.

accentuates the discontinuity of sentiment. Since the "never-resting mind" which assimilates and pervades these particles is Wallace Stevens', however, one would expect these centrifugal parts of a world to cohere about certain ideas of order. Might there even be a dominant idea of order—a jar, so to speak, amid this prolific, polyglot Tennessee? Among Stevens' predecessors in the American tradition, Emerson has most often been accused of self-contradiction, due partly to his aphoristic style. As a student at Harvard, Stevens gained an insight into Emerson's vision that we might apply to his own. Following the essay "Compensation" in his copy of Emerson's *Works*, Stevens wrote, "Hirst, a member of English 5, said, in a lecture on this essay, that Emerson's sentences though apparently distinct and separate were like rays clustering about the single star of his thought."[26]

The very terms *centripetal* and *centrifugal* imply, after all, a centre (to use Stevens' preferred spelling) with respect to which inward and outward movement are oriented. *Centre* is in fact one of Stevens' sacred words, denoting for him some of the same things that *cosmos* meant to the ancient Greeks. His universe of mind and matter, his "central poem," was harmoniously structured according to the principle of analogy or resemblance. The prose section of "Three Academic Pieces" (1947, *NA* 71-82) provides a succinct introduction to this universe. Stevens first proposes, then illustrates the proposition that "in some sense, all things resemble each other" in the physical world. He goes on to explore the nature of the resemblances between two things in reality, between something real and something imagined, and finally between two imaginary things. Resemblance, he maintains, is the realm of metaphor, a realm that points in turn to a sort of meta-metaphor—what he calls elsewhere a "nature that absorbs the mixedness of metaphors" (*OP* 176). This nature is as much a mental as it is a physical entity, for, as he says in "Three Academic Pieces," "What our eyes behold may well be the text of life but one's meditations on the text and the disclosures of these meditations are no less a part of the structure of reality" (*NA* 76). Metaphor has, then, its "aspect of the ideal" (*NA* 81-82), a conclusion which echoes what he had once written to his fiancée on the subject of aphorisms: "You know that the love of maxims is one aspect of Idealism—of which I am not ashamed. . . ."[27]

Metaphor, Stevens emphasizes in "Three Academic Pieces," states an analogical relationship between two things rather than their identity (*NA* 72). However, it takes the rhetorical form of identification: this *is* that. Not content with this conventional mode of identification, Stevens frequently uses the "this is that" and "this and that are one" formulae to suggest an ideal unity between things whose dissimilarity or even opposition renders them intractable to metaphor. The effect is startling when he identifies such things as a man, a woman, and a blackbird (*CP* 93); the poet and his guitar (*CP* 171);

[26] This note appears, together with the date May 1900, in Volume II of the twelve-volume *Works* (Boston: Houghton, 1898), p. 104. The complete set, a gift to Stevens from his mother, is at the Huntington Library.

[27] Letter dated "Sunday Evening" [14 Mar. 1909] to Elsie Kachel (Huntington Library).

order and disorder (*CP* 215); the hero and the general populace (*CP* 251, 289); true and false (*CP* 253); time and space (*CP* 343); poetry and apotheosis (*CP* 378); the captain and his men, the sailor and the sea (*CP* 392); the soldier's war and the poet's (*CP* 407); red and white (*CP* 450); *as* and *is* (*CP* 476); real and unreal (*CP* 485); beginning and end (*CP* 506); Rome and eternity (*CP* 508); God and the imagination (*CP* 524); the poet and the sun (*CP* 532); knowledge and the thing known (*OP* 99); knowing and being (*OP* 101); world and self (*OP* 172); thought and life (*OP* 173); the heavenly creator of earth and the earthly creator of heaven (*OP* 176). Stevens' lecture "Two or Three Ideas" (1951, *OP* 202-16) is organized around three statements of identity whose terms he speculatively rearranges halfway through the piece:

> Now, if the style of a poem and poem itself are one; if the style of the gods and the gods themselves are one; and if the style of men and men themselves are one; and if there is any true relation between these propositions, it might well be the case that the parts of these propositions are interchangeable. Thus, it might be true that the style of a poem and the gods themselves are one; or that the style of the gods and the style of men are one; or that the style of a poem and the style of men are one.
>
> (*OP* 209)

This consolidating habit of mind is manifest in several of the entries in *Sur Plusieurs Beaux Sujects*. We have already seen how Stevens transformed a flower garden, the environment specifically envisioned by the reviewer who said that the art of life "consists mainly in the creation of an environment within which we are of some importance" (Entry 7), into a proprietary realm of imagination—what he would later call his *mundo* (see *CP* 407, *NA* 57). The aphorist who wrote that "Money is a kind of poetry" (*OP* 165) would naturally respond to Pascal's argument that costume and ceremony are also kinds of poetry, used by those in power to enhance their authority (Entry 91). Possibly at the prompting of a book reviewer, Stevens read a passage dealing literally with brightly colored fish as a description of a literary style (Entry 43). Entry 29, dealing with the use of the harp, doubtless found a place in *Sur Plusieurs Beaux Sujects* because he could apply the author's advice to his own poetic instrument, whether he thought of it as a guitar or as the more traditional lyre.

Diverse as the subjects of these passages are—being ostensibly about flower gardens, clothing, fish, and the harp—Stevens identifies all of them with his supreme passion, poetry. Perhaps the most remarkable product of this impulse is Entry 22, where he assimilates to his own métier some rather unpromising material from the catalogue of a rare book collection. This time he supplies the other term of the equation in his annotations (here italicized):

Bibliothèque Henri Beraldi, Première Partie, Livres Anciens des XVIe et XVIIe siècles. Avant-Propos:

. . [.]"Lorsqu'il eut achevé sa tâche, H. B. n'avait-il laissé subsister de son trésor de livres que la quintessence: Le plus beau, le plus rare, le plus pur:" *(a theory of poetry)*

"23. Officium B. Mariae Virginis . . [.] ex officini C . . [.] Plantini 1575 . . . mar. brun, dos orné, plats décorés de rinceaux et de fleurons azurés, avec compartiments mosaïqués. . [. .]" *(the poem itself, the Blessed Virgin being merely the pretext.)*
The subject forms no part. The scholar is not involved. There is only the book, beau, rare et pur.

Stevens has in effect read a complete theory of poetry into the catalogue entries. Analogous to Béraldi's winnowing of his collection is the pure poet's effort to cleanse his work of such "impurities" as didacticism, discursive argument, and even subject matter. The subject, to the extent it survives at all in *la poésie pure*, survives merely as a pretext, like the Blessed Virgin in the splendidly bound *Office*. In Entry 97, to be sure, Stevens entertains the opposite view, that romantic and symbolist theory neglects "one of the most valuable functions of poetry: the illumination of the usual." Had he changed his mind during the fifteen years which separate these entries? Probably not. Rather, they represent the dialogue between imagination and reality to be heard at every stage of his career.

IV

SUR PLUSIEURS BEAUX SUJECTS is characteristically Stevensian in yet another respect. Nowhere except in his poetry and journal do we see him so actively engaged in the process of self-definition. "There is a perfect rout of characters in every man," he observes in his journal immediately after remarking upon the "volatile morality" of trying to live by various maxims, "—and every man is like an actor's trunk, full of strange creatures, new & old" (*SP* 166). Though he goes on to note that an actor and his trunk are two different things, one often has difficulty seeing the actor for the trunk in his poems, where he is continually trying on the masks of dandy and aesthete, burgher and peasant, hero and *l'homme moyen sensuel*. This volatile ethos shows its other side in the commonplace book, where he is consciously the actor or artist. And what sort of artist is he? What are his strengths and weaknesses? How will he be judged by posterity? These are the questions he seems obsessively though indirectly to be putting to himself.

So, at least, one might account for the extraordinary number of excerpts dealing with other writers, artists, musicians, and thinkers. Some entries review individual works, others comment on particular qualities of character, still others assess entire careers. Taken as a group, they constitute a portrait of the kind of poet Stevens aspired to be, if not the kind he always was. They include the little-known as well as the prominent, the unsuccessful as well as the successful: Walter Leaf (Entry 5), Descartes (6), A. Welby Pugin (9), Arnold

14

Bennett (10), Malraux (16), T. S. Eliot (17), Charles M. Doughty (30, 33), Paganini (31), Giraudoux (34), Toulet (35), Hopkins (39), Cézanne (40), Fauré (48), Dali (49), Gay-Lussac (50), Picasso (51, 90), Charpentier (54), Samuel Alexander (59), Pasternak (64), Bartók (76), Klee (78), Walter Scott (88), Santayana (90), A. J. Ayer (92), Matthew Arnold (94), Baudelaire (99), Émile Henriot (103), and Pierre Tal-Coat (104). Among the artistic and intellectual virtues most frequently praised in these entries—and epitomized by figures like Paganini, Toulet, Cézanne, Fauré, Pasternak, and Bartók—are integrity, originality, and unflinching attention to the actual world. Most often singled out for blame is evasion of that world, as in Pugin's attempt to promulgate an exotic architecture, Doughty's improbable characterization, Hopkins' preciosity, and Picasso's excessive intellectualism. Stevens, mindful of similar shortcomings in his own work, apparently chose to preserve these passages as artistic exempla.

How he tried to learn from another's mistakes can be readily seen in the case of Charles Doughty. Returning to a review from which he had already taken one passage, Stevens copied out another in which the English poet is faulted for creating an autonomous world in his poetry (Entry 33). By means of his poetic diction and choice of subject matter, Doughty had achieved an "ideal simplicity of experience" at the expense of "troublesome humanity." In November 1935 Stevens could not have helped but notice the similarity between Anne Treneer's criticism of Doughty, quoted in the review, and that directed against his own work. Reviewing *Ideas of Order* just a month previously, Stanley Burnshaw had dusted off the old chestnut about the "pure poetry" of *Harmonium*, adding that even the sensuous imagery of those early poems has a curiously detached quality. "This is 'scientific,' objectified sensuousness," Burnshaw wrote, "separated from its kernel of fire and allowed to settle, cool off, and harden in the poet's mind until it emerges a strange amazing crystal."[28]

Stevens would in effect endorse Burnshaw's analogy some years later, when he described his poetic *mundo* as the "fat girl" of reality revolving in the crystal of imagination (*CP* 407). In the weeks following the publication of *Ideas of Order*, however, he realized the danger of packaging the world too neatly. "For myself," he had written in his commonplace book while composing the poems in the 1935 collection, "the indefinite, the impersonal, atmospheres and oceans and, above all, the principle of order are precisely what I love . . ." (Entry 19). But writing to his publisher several weeks after the Doughty review, he borrowed a phrase from Treneer to signal the new direction in his thought: "You know, the truth is that I had hardly interested myself in [order] (perhaps as another version of pastoral) when I came across some such phrase as this: 'man's passionate disorder', and I have since been very much interested in disorder" (*L* 300). Though Burnshaw's review undoubtedly helped to shape the character of Stevens' next two books, *Owl's Clover*

<hr>

[28] "Turmoil in the Middle Ground," as reprinted in *Wallace Stevens: The Critical Heritage*, p. 139.

(1936) and *The Man with the Blue Guitar and Other Poems* (1937), Treneer's felicitous phrase and the Doughty review as a whole deserve some of the credit for these experiments in diction and subject matter.

Notwithstanding its heterogeneity and casual character, then, *Sur Plusieurs Beaux Sujects* is the work or work-in-progress of a single poet seriously engaged with the aims, mysteries, and mechanisms of his craft. One might even think of its compiler as a sort of literary persona whose features are already implicit in the title. Here, as so often in the *Collected Poems*, he is a Francophile who values French for its lightness, grace, sound, and color—in short, for its tone.[29] The first and last terms of the title, *Sur . . . Sujects*, align the commonplace book with a familiar type of Stevens poem, the mock-pedantic lecture or treatise. "On the Manner of Addressing Clouds" (1921), "Academic Discourse at Havana" (1923), and "Extracts from Addresses to the Academy of Fine Ideas" (1940) are diverting exercises in a rhetorical mode that also informs weightier poems like "Notes toward a Supreme Fiction."

The word *sujects* warrants particular attention in this regard. When citing the title of the commonplace book, scholars customarily add *sic* to call attention to the apparent solecism or misspelling in the final word. Stevens' mastery of his second language was by no means perfect, to judge from the numerous minor errors in his French excerpts. But if *sujects* is an error for *sujets*, it is an error for which he had historical precedent. French writers of the Renaissance often restored the *c* to words whose Latin roots contain that letter. Stevens was familiar with this archaism and used it in the titles of two poems, "Cy Est Pourtraicte, Madame Ste Ursule, et Les Unze Mille Vierges" (1915) and "Bouquet of Belle Scavoir" (1939).[30] Is *sujects* as legitimate an archaism as *pourtraicte* and *scavoir*? Some French dictionaries authorize the spelling *subjects* as a variant form up to the sixteenth century,[31] and Randle Cotgrave's *Dictionarie of the French and English Tongues* (1611) lists "Suject, ou Sujet" as an acceptable adjectival form.[32] The *Oxford English Dictionary* also lists *suject* as one of several French spellings that precede the modern *sujet*,[33] and Stevens occasionally turned to the *OED* as his ultimate authority, especially when using words of French derivation (see *L* 698-99, 764).

[29] "La légèreté, la grâce, le son et la couleur du français ont eu sur moi une influence indéniable et une influence précieuse," Stevens wrote to René Taupin, who quotes the letter in *L'Influence du symbolisme français sur la poésie américaine (de 1910 à 1920)* (Paris: Honoré Champion, 1929), p. 276.

[30] Renaissance French also preserves the *l* of the Latin root, a practice Stevens adopts in an adage and two of the titles in *From Pieces of Paper*: "Et aultres choses solatieuses" (cf. *OP* 160) and "Aultres Dieux" (Lensing, pp. 168, 171). Similarly archaic is another prospective title or subtitle: "de demeurer en la foy de leur[s] Ancestres" (Lensing, p. 174).

[31] See, for example, Frédéric Godefroy, *Dictionnaire de l'ancienne langue Française* (Paris: Librairie des Sciences et des Arts, 1938), X, 726; and Paul Robert, *Dictionnaire alphabétique et analogique de la langue Française* (Paris: Société du Nouveau Littré, 1966), VI, 397.

[32] London: Adam Islip; reprinted Columbia, S. C.: Univ. of South Carolina Press, 1950.

[33] *The Oxford English Dictionary* (Oxford: Clarendon Press, 1933), X, 20, col. 3.

Perhaps, then, we should give Stevens the benefit of this etymological doubt and dispense with our somewhat patronizing *sic*. Whether authentically archaic or only pseudo-archaic, *Sujects* does help to establish the tone of the commonplace book. Like so many of the poems and letters, *Sur Plusieurs Beaux Sujects* is the work of a serious man who did not want to be taken too seriously—did not want, indeed, to become the subject of scholarly commentary and editions like this one. One might justify ignoring his wishes by pointing to the middle terms of his title. Stevens' commonplace book is, to be sure, less various (*plusieurs*) than Auden's *A Certain World*, whose entries range from *Accidie* to *Writing*; partly for that reason, it is also less inherently appealing (*beaux*). It is nevertheless a fascinating document for the reader who is conscious of what these seedlike subjects became, when they blossomed into the delightful abundance of the *Collected Poems*.

V

THE HENRY E. HUNTINGTON LIBRARY acquired *Sur Plusieurs Beaux Sujects* from Holly Stevens in 1975, together with many other manuscripts, letters, and books that belonged to her father. The commonplace book consists of two exercise notebooks measuring 7¾ x 10⅛ inches. Each notebook contains twenty-four ruled pages, the number of each page being stamped in its upper outside corner. The pages are tied with string to light gray paper covers bearing the titles *SUR PLUSIEURS BEAUX SUJECTS I* and *SUR PLUSIEURS BEAUX SUJECTS II* in hand-written block letters. A small cursive "Cahier I" appears in the upper left-hand corner of the cover of the first notebook, a cursive "Cahier II" in the same place on the second. Cahier I has at least some writing on every page, while the last four pages of Cahier II are blank. There are no cancellations in the notebooks; Stevens wrote the titles and entries in pencil and erased his occasional mistakes.

In the text of *Sur Plusieurs Beaux Sujects* that follows, the reader will find a transcription of each page across from a facsimile of the original. The transcription reproduces the holograph page accurately except for five kinds of alterations. First, a bracketed running head indicates the year or years during which Stevens probably wrote the entries on that page. Second, the page number and lineation of the original, both clearly visible in the facsimile, are not reproduced in the transcription. Third, the entries have been numbered for ease of reference; in the notebooks they are unnumbered but separated by a skipped line. Fourth, periods have been inserted in brackets ([ ]) where they are needed for terminal punctuation or to indicate an ellipsis; Stevens often omits the period at the end of a quotation and typically marks ellipses with two spaced periods. Double brackets ([[ ]]) are used in Entries 24, 69, and 82 to distinguish Stevens' brackets from those used for editorial insertions. Fifth, superscript numerals direct the reader to the footnotes for further information.

The notes supply several kinds of information. Stevens' source is cited in

full whenever it could be found. His departures from his source are also noted; though most of these were inadvertent—the omission or misspelling of a word, for example—he in one instance (Entry 9) deliberately improved upon the punctuation of his source. Where there seem to be errors in an excerpt from an unknown source these are noted as well, though Stevens may simply have copied errors in the original. Where all or part of a passage is in a foreign language, a fairly literal English translation is provided. Thirty entries are in French and one each in Latin and Spanish; another ten entries include short quotations in French or Latin. The notes indicate, finally and most significantly, whether Stevens made use of a given entry in his subsequent writings.

Note

As this edition was about to go to press, I learned the probable source of Stevens' French title. Guillaume Legangneur's *Epigrammes anciens sur plusieurs beaux sujects: Extraicts de l'anthologie des epigrammes grecs par Henry Estienne*, a late-sixteenth-century manuscript, is discussed in the August 1933 issue of the *Bulletin of the Museum of Fine Arts* (Boston), from which Entry 11 is also taken.

Cahier I

SUR PLUSIEURS
BEAUX
SUJECTS
I

Les carrières réussies sont celles qui réalisent dans
l'homme les rêves de l'enfant

                    Je Suis Partout (hebdomadaire Parisien) 12 Mars 1932

                        (Autour d'Aristide Briand)

The felicity of Augustus was often vaunted by
antiquity (with whom success was not so much
a test of merit as itself a merit of the highest
quality)

                    De Quincey   Caesars (Webster's Dict.)

Success as the result of industry in a peasant
ideal.

Success is to be happy with the wise

Nunc me jubet Fortuna expeditius philosophari
    — Sir C. Wren, on losing his appointment
        as Surveyor - General

The above is from a paper by Walter Leaf quoted
by his wife in a memoir which follows his
autobiography in Walter Leaf (Murray, 1932).
The paper seems to have been written after a
considerable reverse in business and illustrates Leaf's
"seriousness and sincerity". It runs, in part, as
follows:
        Every man has a philosophy of life "even
    though it be but to exist as an animal for

1. Les carrières réussies sont celles qui réalisent dans l'homme les rêves de l'enfant[.][1]

    Je Suis Partout (hebdomadaire Parisien[2]) 12 Mars 1932
    (Autour d'Aristide Briand)[3]

2. The felicity of Augustus was often vaunted by antiquity (with whom success was not so much a test of merit as itself a merit of the highest quality)[4]
    De Quincey Caesars (Webster's Dict.)[5]

3. Success as the result of industry is a peasant ideal.[6]

4. Success is to be happy with the wise[.][7]

5. Nunc me jubet Fortuna expeditius philosophari[.][8]
    —Sir C. Wren, on losing his appointment as Surveyor-General[9]

    The above is from a paper by Walter Leaf quoted by his wife in a memoir which follows his autobiography in Walter Leaf (Murray, 1932).[10] The paper seems to have been written after a considerable reverse in business and illustrates Leaf's "seriousness and sincerity". It runs, in part, as follows:

    Every man has a philosophy of life "even though it be but to exist as an animal for

---

[1] "Successful careers are those that realize in the man the dreams of the child."

[2] Sic, for parisien

[3] "Autour d'Aristide Briand," *Je Suis Partout*, 12 Mar. 1932, p. 1, col. 6.

[4] In one edition of Thomas De Quincey's *The Caesars*, the complete sentence reads, "The *felicity* of Augustus was often vaunted by antiquity, (with whom success was not so much a test of merit as itself a merit of the highest quality,) and in no instance was this felicity more conspicuous than in the first act of his entrance upon the political scene" (*Essays in Ancient History and Antiquities*, Vol. VII of *De Quincey's Writings* [Boston: Houghton, Mifflin, 1876], p. 68).

[5] Though Stevens spoke of an "old-fashioned Webster" he consulted at the Hartford Accident and Indemnity Company (*L* 674; cf. *L* 698), no such dictionary remains in the Hartford's law library. Neither have I been able to locate this quotation in any edition of *Webster's International Dictionary of the English Language* or the *New International*.

[6] Samuel French Morse includes this entry among the *Adagia* in *OP* 179, and A. Walton Litz includes it in a separate category of his "Particles of Order: The Unpublished *Adagia*," in *Wallace Stevens: A Celebration* (Princeton: Princeton Univ. Press, 1980), p. 66.

[7] Also included in *OP* 180 and Litz, p. 66.

[8] "Now Fortune decrees that I should philosophize with fewer impediments." In Stevens' source, the Latin quotation is printed in italic type and concludes with a period.

[9] Source: Surveyor-General.

[10] *Walter Leaf 1852-1927: Some Chapters of Autobiography, with a Memoir by Charlotte M. Leaf* (London: John Murray, 1932). The passages which follow are drawn from pp. 161, 163, 166-67.

for the day, with such animal pleasures as chance
may bring him. This is the philosophy of the
wastrel, and from this to the philosophy of a Kant,
a Newton or a St. Francis there is every conceivable
gradation. A man's philosophy is the way in which
he forecasts the future so as to obtain the greatest
satisfaction from it . . . .

The mere effort to think for oneself is one
of the most painful of human efforts; but it is
surely the most essential . . Think, think, think—
these are the three golden rules of human activity.
The progress of the world — the progress of God —
is simply, so far as we can see, the progress of
thought . .

A man should try to give his best thought
to the highest subjects . . Writing is the ultimate test of our honesty to ourselves. . The
thought once worked out to the point of written
record is complete, its work is done. It is a
fragment, a grain added to the thought of the
universe, a grain of sand added to the ever-
growing edifice of God . . "
man's duty is to learn. "

"René Descartes — in the silence of meditation
in the innermost world of man . . pronounced his . . Cogito ergo sum "
                Istituto Cooperium g Religion Ā Liv D Univ P. 193

for the day,[1] with such animal pleasures as chance may bring him. This is the philosophy of the wastrel, and from this to the philosophy of a Kant, a Newton or a St. Francis there is every conceivable gradation. A man's philosophy is the way in which he forecasts the future so as to obtain the greatest satisfaction from it. . . [.]

The mere effort to think for oneself is one of the most painful of human efforts; but it is surely the most essential. . [. .] Think, think, think—these are the three golden rules of human activity. The progress of the world—the progress of God—is simply, so far as we can see, the progress of thought. . [. .]

A man[2] should try to give his best thought to the highest subjects. . [. .] Writing is[3] the ultimate test of our honesty to ourselves. . [. .] The thought once worked out to the point of written record is complete, its work is done.[4] It is a fragment, a grain added to the thought of the universe, a grain of sand added to the ever-growing edifice of God. . [. .]

Man's duty is to *learn*."

6. "René Descartes—in the silence of meditation in the innermost world of man . . [.] pronounced his . . [.] *Cogito ergo sum*."[5]

Idealistic Conception of Religion A Lion O Univ P. 1932[6]

[1] Source: animal for the day,

[2] Source: [. . .] a man

[3] Source: [. . .] writing is

[4] Source: its work done.

[5] Source: Descartes reached certitude by way of observation and direct experience, but it is in the silence of meditation in the innermost world of man that he did so when he at length pronounced his famous *Cogito ergo sum*.

[6] Aline Lion, *The Idealistic Conception of Religion: Vico, Hegel, Gentile* (Oxford: Clarendon Press, 1932), p. 18.

In a notice of The English Flower Garden (by William Robertson, Murray, 15 sd. "one of the great classics of gardening) by Harry Roberts, in the New Statesman for Marshh, 1933, Roberts says,

"The art of peace, as also, I am inclined to think, the art of life itself, consists mainly in the creation of an environment within which we are of some importance. The consciousness of inferiority which characterizes so many people today, destroying their peace and driving them helter-skelter into the barbed-wire entanglements of false philosophies, is due very largely to neglect of this first principle."

Suppose any mann. whose spirit has survived had consulted his contemporaries as to what to do, or what to think, or what music to write, and so on.

"Good common flesh, blood, and mind are beside us here and now, yet we hardly recognize that mistress's real, useful and excellent companionship, hardly consider her presence, thinking to find a matchless beauty in every other neighborhood than our own. It is seldom that the normal is sought with excited zeal, yet it is the normal that is good, and it is the normal that fortunately can most easily be gained. And, the normal is not the average, neither in art, in letters, nor in commerce. The average can never rise to great perfection but the normal can be perfectly expressed

7. In a notice of *The English Flower Garden* (by William Robertson,[1] Murray, 15 Ed. "one of the great classics of gardening["]) by Harry Roberts, in the New Statesman for March 11, 1933,[2] Roberts says,

"The art of play, as also, I am inclined to think, the art of life itself, consists mainly in the creation of an environment within which we are of some importance. The consciousness of inferiority which characterizes so many people today,[3] destroying their peace and driving them helter-skelter into the barbed-wire entanglements of false philosophies, is due very largely to neglect of this first principle."

8. Suppose any man whose spirit has survived had consulted his contemporaries as to what to do, or what to think, or what music to write, and so on.[4]

9. "Good common flesh, blood, and mind are beside us here and now, yet we hardly recognize[5] that mistress's real, useful and excellent companionship, hardly consider her presence, thinking to find a matchless beauty in every other neighbourhood than our own. It is seldom that the normal is sought with excited zeal, yet it is the normal that is good, and it is the normal that fortunately can most easily be gained. And, the normal is not the average, neither in art, in letters, nor in commerce. The average can never rise to great perfection but the normal can be perfectly expressed

[1] Sic, for Robinson
[2] Harry Roberts, "Gardens," rev. of *The English Flower Garden*, 15th ed., by William Robinson, *New Statesman and Nation*, 11 Mar. 1933, p. 289.
[3] Source: characterises so many people to-day,
[4] Also included in *OP* 180 and Litz, p. 67.
[5] Source: recognise

in any activity of man, be it architecture or poetry —
painting or agriculture. Wherever art shines through man's
work, be it in the trim finish of a railway embankment,
in the nice edging of a newly ploughed field, or in the complete expression of an idea in sculpture, it will be seen that
the normal has been fully, and naturally, developed and
that 'Theories of Art' have had little influence. Consider
the works that we call the Classics: they are all founded
in normality and all spring therefrom; and this is so
in regard to all the noble works of man. The beauty of an
English landscape is founded in normal agricultural methods
and has about it all the beauty of English classic literature ... Modernity and newness are as inseparable from
normality, as are the ways of an animal in any
chosen period of its long and slow changing evolution. The normal is not static, it is of the Universe
and with the Universe is forever changes. It is so much
with us that it needs no search to find it, no theory
to teach its presence ... Wherein then did Pugin's
dogma- driven and word - supported theories demanding the revival of Christian architecture fail. True
are the arguments he used to uphold it, and true are
the things he says of that manner of building, when
it was the everyday vernacular. The Theories
proved false ... because they were contrary to
normal development. There is not now, and there never
was, any need to do other in any art or in any
trade than <u>well</u> in an ordinary every - day

in any activity of man, be it architecture or poetry—painting or agriculture. Wherever art shines through man's work, be it in the trim finish of a railway embankment, in the nice edging of a newly ploughed field, or in the complete expression of an idea in sculpture,[1] it will be seen that the normal has been fully and naturally developed and that 'Theories of Art' have had little influence. Consider the works that we call the Classics: they are all founded in normality and all spring therefrom; and this is so in regard to all the noble works of man. The beauty of an English landscape is founded in normal agricultural methods and has about it all the beauty of English classic literature. . . [.] Modernity and newness are as inseparable from normality as are the ways of an animal in any chosen period of its long and slow changing evolution. The Normal is not static, it is[2] of the Universe, and with the Universe it forever changes. It is so much with us that it needs no search to find it, no theory to teach its presence . . .[3] Wherein, then,[4] did Pugin's demon-driven and word-supported theories demanding the revival of Christian architecture fail.[5] True are the arguments he used to uphold it, and true are the things he says of that manner of building, when it was the everyday vernacular. The Theories proved false . . . because they were contrary to normal development. There is not now, and there never was, any need to do other in any art or in any trade than *well* in an ordinary every-day

[1] Source: sculptury,
[2] Source: static it is
[3] Source: nothing omitted between *presence* and *Wherein*, which begins the next paragraph.
[4] Source: Wherein then,
[5] Source: christian architecture fail?

way, the man most fully developed in all his faculties working these in tangible materials will be seen to give his fellows things of such surprising perfection and beauty, as, using words, did Homer and Shakespeare".

A. R. Powys in The London Mercury for May 1933 at p. 63 in a chronicle of Architecture based on The Revival of Christian Architecture, By A. Welby Pugin. 1843.

The mere habit of recording experience increases the chance of not having lived in vain.

Desmond MacCarthy a propos Arnold Bennett's Journal in Life & Letters for June 1933 p. 135

"Therefore it has seemed to me, Sire, that the best science we can pursue (after the fear of God) is to keep ourselves merry, by following genteel exercises"

La Venerie, Jacques du Fouilloux, quoted in a note, Three French Humanists in Bulletin of the Museum of Fine Arts (Boston) XXXI, 57, August 1933.

"Delete the fear of God.

".. worlds of form and discipline, worlds created accurately, out of enlightened personality" p.132 Without My Cloak. Kate O'Brien

way. The man most fully developed in all his faculties working thus in tangible materials will be seen to give his fellows things of such surprising perfection and beauty as, using words, did Homer[1] and Shakespeare".

A. R. Powys in The London Mercury for May 1933 at p. 63 in a chronicle of Architecture based on The Revival of Christian Architecture, By A. Welby Pugin, 1843.[2]

10. The mere[3] habit of recording experience increases the chance of not having lived in vain.

Desmond MacCarthy apropos Arnold Bennett's *Journal* in Life & Letters for June 1933, p. 135[4]

11. "Therefore it has seemed to me, Sire, that the best science we can pursue (after the fear of God) is to keep ourselves merry by following genteel exercises[.]"

La Venerie, Jacques du Fouilloux, quoted in a note, Three French Humanists in Bulletin of the Museum of Fine Arts (Boston) XXXI, 57, August, 1933.[5]

Delete the fear of God.

12. . . [.] "worlds of form and discipline, worlds created accurately out of enlightened personality"[6] p. 132

Without My Cloak: Kate O'Brien[7]

---

[1] Source: did, Homer

[2] A. R. Powys, rev. of *The Revival of Christian Architecture*, by A. Welby Pugin, *London Mercury*, 28 (May 1933), 63-64.

[3] Source: [. . .] the mere

[4] Desmond MacCarthy, "A Critic's Daybook," *Life and Letters*, 9 (June 1933), 135.

[5] H[enry] P[reston] R[ossiter], "Three French Humanists," *Bulletin of the Museum of Fine Arts* (Boston), 31 (Aug. 1933), 57.

[6] Source: personality [. . .].

[7] Kate O'Brien, *Without My Cloak* (London: Heinemann, 1931), pp. 131-32; the following excerpt is from p. 455.

.. "it is only by breaking a few conventions
that an intelligent young man can learn their
irreplaceable value"

        id ; p. 955

In the long run the truth does not
matter.

"Classical mythology cannot be expelled from
English poetic consciousness .. The Irish poets
almost succeeded in beguiling everyone with
Celtic divinities and symbols .. The ancient
Hebrew chronicles and myths are an integral
part of the religious consciousness of England"
       New Statesman, Jan. 13, 1934 p. 48, a
         note on Mr. Sturge Moore as "a very
     individual medium"

It should be said of poetry that it is essentially romantic as if one were recognizing the
truth about poetry for the first time. Although
the romantic is referred to most often, in a
pejorative sense, this sense 'attaches, or should
attach, not to the romantic in general but
to some phase of the romantic that has
become stale. Just as there is always a
romantic that is potent, so there is always
a romantic that is impotent.

. . [.] "it is only by breaking a few conventions that an intelligent young man can learn their irreplaceable value[.]"
    id; p. 455[1]

13. In the long run the truth does not matter[.][2]

14. "Classical mythology cannot be expelled from English poetic consciousness. . [. .] The Irish poets almost succeeded in beguiling everyone with Celtic divinities and symbols. . [. .] The ancient Hebrew chronicles and myths are an integral part of the religious consciousness of England[.]"
    New Statesman, Jan. 13, 1934 p. 48, a note on Mr. Sturge Moore as "a very individual medium"[3]

15. It should be said of poetry that it is essentially romantic as if one were recognizing the truth about poetry for the first time. Although the romantic is referred to, most often, in a pejorative sense, this sense attaches, or should attach, not to the romantic in general but to some phase of the romantic that has become stale. Just as there is always a romantic that is potent, so there is always a romantic that is impotent.[4]

[1] id: for idem

[2] Also included in *OP* 180 and Litz, p. 67.

[3] Austin Clarke, "Mr. Sturge Moore," rev. of *The Poems of T. Sturge Moore*, Vol. IV, *New Statesman and Nation*, 13 Jan. 1934, p. 48.

[4] Also in *OP* 180 and Litz, p. 67. Compare Stevens' "Sailing after Lunch" (1935, *CP* 120-21) and letters to Ronald Lane Latimer of 12 Mar. 1935 (*L* 276-77) and T. C. Wilson of 25 Mar. 1935 (*L* 278-79).

Of a wore by André Malraux:
"Au total, l'ouvrage ne laisse pas en
repos le goût ni l'esprit"
André Thérive, Le Temps. 29-6-33.

"Mr. Eliot, a critic of Manzanilla siccity
of bouquet, . ."
Osbert Burdett No 173 Lond. Mercury 471

But what can philosophy do except
amiably reflect the philosopher's nature?
Thomas Sergeant Perry: Letters.
(To W. James, May 5, 1909) p.48

The philosopher could not love the indefinite
and impersonal principle of order pervading
the universe, any more than he could love atmospheres or oceans.
Storrs, Divine Origin of Christianity
For myself, the indefinite, the impersonal, atmospheres and oceans and, above all, the principle of order are precisely what I love; and
I dont see why, for a philosopher, they should
not be the ultimate amorata. The premise
to Storrs is that the universe is explicable only
in terms of humanity.

".. the great interests of man: air and light,

[1934]

16. Of a novel by André Malraux:
   "Au total,[1] l'ouvrage ne laisse pas en repos le goût ni l'esprit[.]"[2]
   André Thérive, Le Temps, 29-6-33.[3]

17. "Mr. Eliot, a critic of Manzanilla siccity of bouquet, . . [.]"[4]
   Osbert Burdett No 173 Lond. Mercury 471[5]

18. But what can philosophy do except amiably reflect the philosopher's nature?
   Thomas Sergeant Perry: Letters. (To W. James, May 5, 1909) p. 48[6]

19. The philosopher could not love the indefinite and impersonal principle of order pervading the universe, any more than he could love atmospheres or oceans.
   Storrs, Divine Origin of Christianity[7]

For myself, the indefinite, the impersonal, atmospheres and oceans and, above all, the principle of order are precisely what I love; and I dont see why, for a philosopher, they should not be the ultimate inamorata. The premise to Storrs is that the universe is explicable only in terms of humanity.

20. ". .[.] the great interests of man: air and light,

[1] Source: Or, au total,

[2] "On the whole, the work satisfies neither the taste nor the intellect."

[3] André Thérive, rev. of *L'Affaire Courilof*, by Irène Nemirovsky, and *La Condition humaine*, by André Malraux, *Le Temps*, 29 June 1933, p. 3, col. 5.

[4] In a letter to Allen Tate of 6 July 1943 (now in the Allen Tate Papers, Princeton University Library), Stevens writes, "My rather pulpy poem doesn't take on a 'Manzanillan siccity' merely because it has been translated into Spanish." He refers to "Discourse in a Cantina at Havana," which had been translated for *Revista de avance* (Havana), 15 Nov. 1929, pp. 326-27. For Stevens' approval of Braque's "siccity," see *L* 548.

[5] Osbert Burdett, rev. of *Studies French and English*, by F. L. Lucas, and seven other books, *London Mercury*, 29 (Mar. 1934), 471.

[6] *Selections from the Letters of Thomas Sergeant Perry*, ed. Edwin Arlington Robinson (New York: Macmillan, 1929), p. 48. Stevens is apparently paraphrasing Perry in his letter to Barbara Church of 30 Nov. 1951, where he writes, "Tom Sergeant [sic], an eminent Bostonian, said that philosophy is a thing in which the philosopher exhibits his natural amiability. I like that attitude" (*L* 734).

[7] Richard S. Storrs, *The Divine Origin of Christianity Indicated by Its Historical Effects* (New York: Anson D. F. Randolph, 1884), p. 89.

the joy of having a body, the voluptuousness of looking."
                    Maria Rossi in *Life*.

Miss Yeats, who published one of Dr. Rossi's works,
gave me his address. He wrote to me in April, 1934,
from Reggio Emilia,

"I don't think indeed man has only
such interests; I meant to say that amongst
human interests, the simple pleasures of life
— living pure, as it were — have a paramount
importance ... The glory and glamour of the
world is enough in itself to make man happy
with his destiny.. Poetry and pleasure alike
have something elemental in themselves.. But
this implies .. that reality is further on ...
Yes, a Pagan if you like. But don't forget
.. there was the inscrutable Ananke. Call
it destiny, call it God, call it predestination
— it comes all alike. It gives a sense to the
marvelous spectacle of the world .."

Inscrutable is Dr. Rossi's magnificent word and
Ananke is necessity or fate personified; the *saeva
Necessitas* of Horace Odes Book I No.35, to For-
tune:

"Inexorable Necessity always marches before thee, holding in her brazen hand huge
spikes and wedges .." it

the joy of having a body, the voluptuousness of looking."
　　　　Mario Rossi in *Swift*.[1]

Miss Yeats, who published one of Dr. Rossi's works, gave me his address. He wrote to me in April, 1934, from Reggio Emilia,

"I dont think indeed man has only[2] such interests. I meant to say that amongst human interests, the simple pleasures of life—living pure, as it were—have a paramount importance. . [. .] The glory[3] and glamour of the world is enough in itself to make man happy with his destiny. . [. .] Poetry and pleasure alike have something elemental in themselves. . [. .] But this implies . . [.] that reality is further on. . [. .] Yes, a Pagan if you like. But dont forget . . [.] there[4] was the imperscrutable Ananke.[5] Call it destiny, call it God, call it predestination—it comes all alike. It gives a sense to the marvelous[6] spectacle of the world. . [. .]"
Imperscrutable is Dr. Rossi's magnificent word and Ananke is necessity or fate personified: the saeva Necessitas of Horace Odes Book I No. 35, to Fortune:

"Inexorable Necessity always marches before thee, holding in her brazen hand huge spikes and wedges . . [.]" etc

---

[1] Stevens used this quotation as the epigraph to "Evening without Angels," first published in October 1934 (*CP* 136-38). When he looked into Rossi and J. M. Hone's *Swift, or The Egotist* (London: Gollancz, 1934) in 1940, he realized he had not taken the epigraph from that book (*L* 347). He speculated that it might have come from *Life and Letters*, where George Lensing has in fact located it, in Rossi's "Essay on the Character of Swift," 8 (Sept. 1932), 356 (*Wallace Stevens: A Poet's Growth*, p. 215). The essay prompted Stevens to write to Rossi in 1934, eliciting the reply he excerpts below. Rossi's letter, dated 17 Apr. 1934, has apparently been lost, though it is recorded on microfilm at the Dartmouth College Library. In 1940 Stevens loaned the letter to Hi Simons (see *L* 347), who made a "true copy" now in the Hi Simons Papers, University of Chicago Library.

[2] Source: *only*

[3] Source: But the glory

[4] Source: forget over and above Jove and the Olympus [sic] there

[5] The term *Ananke* appears in "Like Decorations in a Nigger Cemetery," XII (1935, *CP* 152), "The Greenest Continent," VIII (1936, *OP* 59), and a draft of "Examination of the Hero in a Time of War," I (about 1941, *OP* 83). In all of these, it personifies fate or necessity. As a "thing created by the imagination" and surrogate object of religious belief, Ananke became in 1940 the immediate precursor of Stevens' supreme fiction (*L* 370). Freud's *The Future of an Illusion* supplied him with another meaning for Ananke when he was preparing his 1941 lecture, "The Noble Rider and the Sound of Words." On p. 93 of his copy of that book (London: Hogarth, 1928), the same page from which he took Freud's "voice of the intellect" remark (*NA* 15), he glossed Freud's argument in the margin: "ἀνάγκη = external reality." This book is at the University of Massachusetts Library.

[6] Source: marvellous

Ex Divina Pulchritudine esse omnium Derivatur, and also all poetry. And in reflecting on this think of it in connection with the association of poetry and pleasure and also, in connection with l'instinct du bonheur. If happiness is in our selves, divine pulchritudo is in our selves and poetry is a revelation or a contact.

Bibliothèque Henri Beraldi, Première Partie, Livres Anciens des XVIᵉ et XVIIᵉ siècles. Avant-Propos:

.. `Lorsqu'il eut achevé sa tâche, H. B. n'avait-il laissé subsister de son trésor de livres que la quintessence: Le plus beau, le plus rare, le plus pur." (a theory of poetry)

"23. Officium B. Mariae Virginis ..
y Officini C.. Plantini 1575 ... mar.brun, dos orné, plats décorés de rinceaux et de fleurons azurés, avec compartiments mosaïqués .. (the poem itself, the Blessed Virgin being merely the pretext.)
The subject forms no part. The scholar is not involved. There is only the book, beau, rare et pur.

"Yes, everyday things are important, too! They mean as much as Scripture, for where would Maimonides have been without his mother's

21. Ex Divina Pulchritudine esse omnium Derivatur,[1] and, above all, poetry. And in reflecting on this think of it in connection with the association of poetry and pleasure and, also, in connection with l'instinct du bonheur.[2] If happiness is in our selves, divine pulchritude is in our selves and poetry is a revelation or a contact.

22. Bibliothèque Henri Beraldi, Première Partie, Livres Anciens des XVIᵉ et XVIIᵉ siècles.[3] Avant-Propos:
    . . [.] "Lorsqu'il[4] eut achevé sa tâche, H. B.[5] n'avait-il laissé subsister de son trésor de livres que la quintessence: Le plus beau, le plus rare, le plus pur:"[6] (a theory of poetry)
        "23. Officium B. Mariae Virginis . . [.] ex officini C . . [.] Plantini 1575[7] . . . mar. brun, dos orné, plats décorés de rinceaux et de fleurons azurés, avec compartiments mosaïqués. . [. .]"[8] (the poem itself, the Blessed Virgin being merely the pretext.)
    The subject forms no part. The scholar is not involved. There is only the book, beau, rare et pur.

23. "Yes, everyday things are important, too: they mean as much as Scripture, for where would Maimonides have been without his mother's

---

[1] "From Divine Beauty is derived the existence of all things."

[2] "the instinct for happiness"

[3] *Bibliothèque Henri Béraldi, première partie: Livres anciens des XVIᵉ et XVIIᵉ siècles* (Paris: É. Ader, 1934), pp. 1, 13.

[4] Source: Aussi, lorsqu'il

[5] Source: Henri Beraldi

[6] Source: *Le plus beau . . . pur* in italic type, followed by a period. Stevens used one of these phrases in "The Blue Buildings in the Summer Air" (1938): "Go, mouse, go nibble at Lenin in his tomb. / Are you not le plus pur, you ancient one?" (*CP* 217). He may have been recalling another when he entitled one of his poems "Les Plus Belles Pages" (1941, *CP* 244).

[7] Source: *ex officina Christophori Plantini*, 1575;

[8] "Library of Henri Béraldi, First Part, Old Books of the Sixteenth and Seventeenth Centuries, Preface:
    '. . . When he had finished his task, H. B. had retained of his trove of books only the quintessence: the most beautiful, the most rare, the most pure' (a theory of poetry).
    '23. Office of the B. Virgin Mary . . . from the workshop of C. Plantini, 1575 . . . brown morocco, ornamented spine, boards decorated with foliage and blue-tinted floral ornaments, with inlaid partitions. . . .'"

milk?"

The Salzburg Tales; Christina Stead, p. 113.

"The profane multitude I hate, and only consecrate
my strange Poems to those searching spirits,
whom learning hath made noble, and nobility
sacred"., [That plainness should be the
special ornament of Poesy.] "were the plain
way to barbarism, and to make the Ass
proud of his ears; to take away strength
from Lions, and give Camels horns".
George Chapman

Scipion. —   Mais pour que je me délecte
d'un melon particulièrement doux, faut-
il que je m'intéresse au jardinier et supporte ses commérages? Tais-toi et me
laisse en paix contempler ce grand spectacle.
Jean Schlumberger, Dialogues
des Ombres Pendant Le Combat (Between
Scipio and Terence) La Nouvelle Revue Française,
1er Juillet 1919, no 70.

"It was pleasant, this business of being charming and rather amusing and making
love light-heartedly. Financially it was
proving enormously profitable to all concerned, and infinitely more worth while

milk?''
The Salzburg Tales, Christina Stead, p. 113.[1]

24. "The profane multitude I hate, and only consecrate my strange Poems to these searching spirits, whom learning hath made noble, and nobility sacred". . [. .] [That plainness should be the special ornament of Poesy,] "were the plain way to barbarism,[2] and to make the Ass proud of his ears; to take away strength from Lions, and give Camels horns".
George Chapman[3]

25.   Scipion.—Mais[4] parce que je me délecte d'un melon particulièrement doux, faut-il que je m'intéresse au jardinier et supporte ses commérages? Tais-toi et me laisse en paix contempler ce grand spectacle.[5]

Jean Schlumberger, Dialogues Des Ombres Pendant Le Combat (Between Scipio and Terence), La Nouvelle Revue Française, 1er Juillet 1919, No 70.[6]

26. "It was pleasant, this business of being charming and rather amusing and making love light-heartedly. Financially it was proving enormously profitable to all concerned, and infinitely more worth while

---

[1] Christina Stead, *The Salzburg Tales* (London: Peter Davies, 1934), p. 113.

[2] Compare "An Ordinary Evening in New Haven," IV (1949): "The plainness of plain things is savagery . . ." (*CP* 467).

[3] This excerpt is from Chapman's dedicatory epistle to *Ovids Banquet of Sence*. Stevens' source is unknown; in the authoritative *Poems of George Chapman*, ed. Phyllis Brooks Bartlett (New York: Modern Language Association of America, 1941), the passage reads,

> . . . The prophane multitude I hate, & onlie consecrate my strange Poems to these serching spirits, whom learning hath made noble, and nobilitie sacred. . . . But that Poesie should be as peruiall as Oratorie, and plainnes her speciall ornament, were the plaine way to barbarisme: and to make the Asse runne proude of his eares; to take away strength from Lyons, and giue Cammels hornes.

> (p. 49)

As Stevens may have realized (cf. Entry 20), Chapman's opening clause echoes Horace's Ode III.i, which begins, "Odi profanum vulgus . . ."

[4] Source: Scipion.—[. . .] Mais

[5] "Scipio.—. . . But because I am enjoying an especially sweet melon, must I take an interest in the gardener and endure his gossip? Be quiet and leave me to contemplate this grand spectacle in peace."

[6] Jean Schlumberger, "Dialogues des ombres pendant le combat," *La Nouvelle Revue Française*, 1 July 1919, p. 215.

than standing in tights before a dark curtain,
protesting to few people in the stalls that all
our yesterdays have lighted fools the way to
dusty death."

　　　　Gerald: A Portrait by Daphne
　　　　du Maurier p. 121 (Gerald du
　　　　Maurier)

"Should the philosopher concern himself with public affairs, or should he retire to a mountain-top
and meditate. Philosophers have always been divided into two schools by this problem. Those who
were friends of rulers composed maxims for the
management of the State; those who were not,
consoled themselves with theories about the universe."

　　　　Bertrand Russell, The New States-
　　　　man, June 1, 1935.

"I am worried by thoughts of a war oftener than
by thoughts of my own death, yet the line to be adopted over both these nuisances is the same. One must
behave as if one is immortal, and as if civilization
is eternal. Both statements are false — I shall not
survive, no more will the great globe itself — both of
them must be assumed to be true if we are to
go on eating and working and travelling,
and keep open a few breathing holes for the
human spirit. And though I am not a public

than standing in tights before a dark curtain, protesting to five people in the stalls that all our yesterdays have lighted fools the way to dusty death".

Gerald: A Portrait by Daphne du Maurier p. 121 (Gerald du Maurier)[1]

27. "Should[2] the philosopher concern himself with public affairs, or should he retire to a mountain-top and meditate.[3] Philosophers have always been divided into two schools by this problem. Those who were friends of rulers composed maxims for the management of the State; those who were not, consoled themselves with theories about the universe."
Bertrand Russell, The New Statesman, June 1, 1935.[4]

28. "I am worried by thoughts of a war oftener than by thoughts of my own death, yet the line to be adopted over both these nuisances is the same. One must behave as if one is immortal, and as if civilization is eternal. Both statements are false—I shall not survive, no more will the great globe itself—both of them must be assumed to be true if we are to go on eating and working and travelling, and keep open a few breathing holes for the human spirit. Although I am not a public

---

[1] Daphne du Maurier, *Gerald: A Portrait* (Garden City: Doubleday, 1935), pp. 115-16.

[2] Source: A week of political excitements—Hitler's speech, the Abyssinian trouble, the increase in our air force, and so on—raises once more the perpetual question: should

[3] Source: mcditate?

[4] Bertrand Russell, "A Weekly Diary," *New Statesman and Nation*, 1 June 1935, p. 798.

speaker; I wanted to come to Paris to say this, whatever our various remedies for the present evils — and
we are sure to differ — we all believe in courage. If
a writer is courageous and sensitive he has to my mind
fulfilled his public calling. He has helped to rally
humanity in the presence of catastrophe."

      E. M. Forster, Liberty in England,
   an address at the Congrès International des Écrivains at
  Paris, June 21, 1935. London Mercury, August 1935.

Lavignac exprime l'opinion classique lorsqu'il écrit:
"La harpe ne doit apparaître que lorsque son emploi
est motivé par son double caractère éthéré et hiératique.. Son effet est des plus saisissants et des
plus poétiques lorsqu'on sait le <u>tenir</u> en réserve."
                  Marianne

"In the superficial sense that Doughty kept
himself out of his poetry he is, of course, objective
enough; but in the sense of being able to imagine
and create a world of persons in whose existence
we believe and in whose vicissitudes we are concerned Doughty was not objective at all. He is
remote, which is quite different matter."
          Times Lit. Supp. Nov. 9. 1935,
          on Doughty's Influence To-Day

speaker, I wanted to come to Paris to say this. Whatever our various remedies for the present evils—and we are sure to differ—we all believe in courage. If a writer is courageous and sensitive he has to my mind fulfilled his public calling. He has helped to rally humanity in the presence of catastrophe."

E. M. Forster, Liberty In England, an address at the Congrès International des Ecrivains at Paris, June 21, 1935, London Mercury August 1935.[1]

29. Lavignac exprime l'opinion classique lorsqu'il écrit: "La harpe ne doit apparaître que lorsque son emploi est motivé par son double caractère éthéré et hiératique. . Son effet[2] est des plus saisissants et des plus poétiques lorsqu'on sait *le tenir en réserve*".[3]

Marianne[4]

30. "In the superficial sense that Doughty kept himself out of his poetry he is, of course, objective enough; but in the sense of being able to imagine and create a world of persons in whose existence we believe and in whose vicissitudes we are concerned Doughty was not objective at all. He is remote; which is a quite different matter."

Times Lit. Supp. Nov. 9, 1935, on Doughty's Influence To-Day[5]

---

[1] E. M. Forster, "Liberty in England," *London Mercury*, 32 (Aug. 1935), 331.

[2] Source: hiératique . . . Son effet

[3] "Lavignac expresses the traditional opinion when he writes: 'The harp ought to appear only when its use is justified by its twofold character, ethereal and hieratic. . . . Its effect is the more thrilling and poetic when one knows how *to keep it in reserve*.'"

[4] Jean-Richard Bloch, "La Harpe," *Marianne*, 18 Sept. 1935, p. 5, col. 3.

[5] "Doughty as an Influence To-Day: An Over-Simple Creed," rev. of *Charles M. Doughty: A Study of His Prose and Verse*, by Anne Treneer; and *Selected Passages from "The Dawn in Britain" of Charles Doughty*, ed. Barker Fairley, *Times Literary Supplement*, 9 Nov. 1935, p. 716, col. 3.

Préoccupé déjà de chercher sur son instrument de nouveaux effets... Paganini — comprenant bien qu'en suivant la même voie que ses devanciers, il ne pouvait arriver au plus qu'à les égaler, il a su chercher et trouver des procédés inconnus ; il s'est fait une technique entièrement nouvelle.

Sous le règne des grands principes, tout ce qui est sous le ciel était à tous.

Confucius

From a note on Doughty, in the Times Literary Supplement, Nov. 9, 1935. He abstracts:

"Miss Treneer ... in her final summing up .. puts 'it' .. :-

'Could he have presented the passionate disorder in the hearts of men as he presents the passionate heat at the core of the earth he would also have been a great tragic poet. As it is, there is something in Doughty, call it moral fibre, or a sense of rectitude, or of noble reserve, which limited his field when treating of what is human in poetry'.

To me Keats's antithesis, Doughty, as poet belonged to the 'egotistical sublime' and 'the men of character'. That is no defect in itself .. He belonged to the 'egotistical sublime' because he insisted on creating a world for himself in his

31. Preoccupé dejà[1] de chercher sur son instrument de nouveaux effets . . [.]
Paganini—comprenant bien qu'en suivant la même voie que ses devanciers, il ne pouvait arriver au plus qu'a les egaler,[2] il a su chercher
et trouver des procédés inconnus; il s'est fait une technique entiere-
ment nouvelle.[3]

32. Sous le règne des grands principes, tout ce qui est sous le ciel était à tous.[4]
Confucius

33. From a note on Doughty in the Times Literary Supplement, Nov. 9, 1935.[5]
See above:

"Miss Treneer . . [.] in her final summing up . . [.] puts it . . [.]:—[6]

'Could he have presented the passionate disorder in the hearts of men[7]
as he presents the passionate heat at the core of the earth he would also
have been a great tragic poet. As it is, there is something in Doughty, call it
moral fibre, or a sense of rectitude, or of noble reserve, which limited his
field when treating of what is human in poetry'.

To use Keats's antithesis, Doughty as poet belonged to the 'egotistical
sublime' and 'the men of character'.[8] That is no defect in itself[9]. . . [.] He
belonged to the 'egotistical sublime' because he insisted on creating a
world for himself in his

---

[1] Sic, for Préoccupé déjà

[2] Sic, for qu'à les égaler,

[3] Sic, for entièrement nouvelle. "Already preoccupied with seeking new effects on his instrument . . . Paganini, well aware that by following the same path as his predecessors he could man-
age only to equal them, knew how to search for and find methods unknown; he created for
himself a technique altogether new." Paganini's Caprice No. 9 in E major, op. 1, is listed in Michael
O. Stegman, "Wallace Stevens and Music: A Discography of Stevens' Phonograph Record Collection," *Wallace Stevens Journal*, 3 (Fall 1979), 91.

[4] This translates the first part of a sentence in the *Li Yun* chapter of the Confucian classic *Li Ji* (*Li
Chi* in the Wade-Giles system):"Da dao zhi xing ye, tian xia wei gong . . ." (Sec. I.2). James Legge
renders it, "When the Grand course was pursued, a public and common spirit ruled all under the
sky . . ." (*Li Chi: Book of Rites* [New Hyde Park, N.Y.: University Books, 1967], I, 364). Stevens'
source is unknown; it does not follow the better-known French translations by J. M. Callery
(1833) or Séraphin Couvreur (1913).

[5] Source as for Entry 30, cols. 3-4.

[6] Source: [. . .] Miss Treneer [. . .] In her final summing up she puts it more discreetly:—
Treneer's words are set in smaller type rather than being set off by quotation marks.

[7] Stevens remembered this phrase as "man's passionate disorder" in a letter to Ronald Lane
Latimer of 10 Dec. 1935 (*L* 300); also see the Introduction, pp. 15-16.

[8] Source: character."

[9] Source: defect, in itself.

poetry ... with most of the troublesome humanity left out ... He is manifestly in pursuit of an ideal simplicity of experience ... Outside that extreme of simplicity, his touch is faltering. One might almost say that he was involved in a dilemma. In dealing with any less simple human material he was bound to abandon either his style or his characters, because that poetic diction of his is not adequate to human behaviour as we know it."

"Lorsqu'il entreprend avec ses personnages des promenades sentimentales, M. Girandoux, nous le savons, s'oriente souvent et malgré lui vers la préciosité. Il s'abandonne à ses richesses. Il s'attarde dans un univers abstrait plein de chausse-trapes, d'allées à surprises et de bosquets imprévus. C'est la lumière de son esprit qui fait miroiter ces paysages fallacieux et non la bonne et franche lumière du jour. Mais lorsqu' il s'éloigne de ces figurines passagères, lorsqu'il les dépasse, lorsqu'il oublie leurs anecdotes et se trouve en présence du destin, les choses changent. Son sentiment se simplifie, le rythme n'est plus le même, la poésie prend son essor. Des paroles vraies sont dites, qui viennent de loin et qui vont loin. Certaines clartés frappantes surgissent du texte. Les phrases ont une plénitude

poetry . . [.] with most of the troublesome humanity left out. . [. .] He is manifestly in pursuit of an ideal simplicity of experience. . [. .] Outside that extreme of simplicity his[1] touch is faltering. One might almost say that he was involved in a dilemma. In dealing with any less simple human material he was bound to abandon either his style or his characters, because that poetic diction of his is not adequate to human behaviour as we know it."

34. "Lorsqu'il entreprend avec ses personnages des promenades sentimentales, M. Giraudoux, nous le savons, s'oriente souvent et malgré lui vers la préciosité. Il s'abandonne à ses richesses. Il s'attarde dans un univers abstrait plein de chausse-trapes, d'allées à surprises et de bosquets imprévus. C'est la lumière de son esprit qui fait miroiter ces paysages fallacieux et non la bonne et franche lumière du jour. Mais, lorsqu'il[2] s'éloigne de ces figurines passagères, lorsqu'il les depasse,[3] lorsqu'il oublie leurs anecdotes et se trouve en présence du destin, les choses changent. Son sentiment se simplifie, le rythme n'est plus le même, la poésie prend son essor. Des paroles vraies sont dites, qui viennent de loin et qui vont loin. Certaines clartés frappantes surgissent du texte. Les phrases ont une plénitude

[1] Source: simplicity, his
[2] Source: Mais lorsqu'il
[3] Source: dépasse,

étrange. Il semble, dans ces instants-là, que l'atmosphère
devienne à la fois plus calme et plus sonore"

   M. Pierre Brisson in Le Figaro à propos La
Guerre de Troie n'aura pas lieu by M. Jean Giraudoux
presented Nov. 21. 1935 at Théâtre de l'Athénée.

"Toulet, qui souhaitait probablement vivre avec le souvenir
de certaines collections du Louvre, qu'il avait tant de
fois visitées, me priait de lui expédier des cartes
postales... "Celles que je desire sont... 2° Statues
antiques sans trop chercher les plus belles". Je me
suis souvent représenté Toulet traçant ces mots. Il
est là tout entier, dans cet amour non point d'une
splendeur surhumaine, mais de cette beauté résultant
de l'équilibre des forces naturelles"
   Francis Carco, Amitié Avec Toulet

"Contemporary music is a portrait of the present as
seen through the lens of the past and as painted in oils
whose qualities have already been thoroughly tested,
modern music is a prophecy – an art still suffering
from growing-pains, destined to attain its full stature
at some future day, when it will be recognized as
springing from its own."
   A Note On Arnold Shoenberg, in The Musical
   Quarterly, by D. J. Bach, for Jan. 1936

"Poetry creates a fictitious existence in an egoistic

étrange. Il semble, dans ces instants-là, que l'atmosphère devienne à la fois plus calme et plus sonore[.]"[1]

M. Pierre Brisson in Le Figaro à propos La Guerre de Troie n'aura pas lieu by M. Jean Giraudoux presented Nov. 21, 1935 at Théatre de l'Athénée.[2]

35. "Toulet, qui souhaitait probablement vivre avec le souvenir de certaines collections du Louvre, qu'il avait tant de fois visitées, me priait de lui expédier des cartes postales. . [. .] 'Celles que je desire[3] sont . . [.] 2° Statues antiques sans trops[4] chercher les plus belles'. . [. .] Je me suis souvent représenté Toulet traçant ces mots. Il est là tout entier, dans cet amour non point d'une splendeur surhumaine, mais de cette beauté résultant de l'equilibre des forces naturelles"[5]

Francis Carco, Amitié Avec Toulet[6]

36. "*Contemporary*[7] music is a portrait of the present as seen through the lens of the past and as painted in oils whose qualities have already been thoroughly tested; *modern* music is a prophecy—an art still suffering from growing-pains, destined to attain its full stature at some future day, when it will be[8] recognized as springing from our own."

A Note On Arnold Shoenberg,[9] in The Musical Quarterly, by D. J. Bach, for Jan. 1936[10]

37. Poetry creates a fictitious existence on an exquisite

---

[1] "When he attempts sentimental excursions with his characters, M. Giraudoux, we know, often turns despite himself toward preciosity. He surrenders himself to its riches. He dallies in an abstract universe, full of snares, unforeseen paths, and unexpected thickets. It is the radiance of his mind that causes these fallacious landscapes to glisten, and not the good and honest light of day. But when he departs from these transitory figurines, when he goes beyond them, when he forgets their anecdotes and finds himself in the presence of destiny, things change. His feeling becomes simple, the rhythm is no longer the same, the poetry takes wing. Some genuine words are spoken, which come from afar and which go a long way. Certain striking clarities emerge from the text. The sentences have a strange fullness. It seems, at such moments, that the atmosphere becomes simultaneously more tranquil and more resonant."

[2] Pierre Brisson, "Athénée: *La Guerre de Troie n'aura pas lieu*, pièce en deux actes de M. Jean Giraudoux," *Le Figaro*, 24 Nov. 1935, p. 5, cols. 1-2.

[3] Source: désire

[4] Source: trop

[5] Source: l'équilibre des forces naturelles [. . .]. "Toulet, who probably wanted to live with the memory of certain collections of the Louvre that he had so often visited, asked me to send him post cards. . . .'The ones I want are . . . , second, ancient statues without undue searching for the most beautiful. . . .' I have often imagined Toulet writing these words. He is there epitomized, in that love not of superhuman splendor but of that beauty resulting from the balance of natural forces. . . ."

[6] Francis Carco, *Amitié avec Toulet* (Paris: Le Divan, 1934), pp. 25-27. Stevens mentions Paul-Jean Toulet in "Like Decorations in a Nigger Cemetery," XV (1935, *CP* 153), and Carco in a letter to Ronald Lane Latimer of 24 Jan. 1936 (*L* 306). He owned copies of Toulet's *Le Mariage de Don*

plane. This definition must vary, as the plane
varies, an exquisite plane being merely "illustrative.

It would be truer to say that Chinese painting is
a branch of poetry, and that calligraphy is the
medium of both.

W. B. Honey, The Eumorfopoulos Collection
Apollo, Oct. 1936, p. 204

". . . or see his false start as a poet reaching its
climax in Heaven - Haven (1866) . . The point about
Heaven - Haven and all his poems of that kind is not
so much that they are bad – some indeed are exquisite
– as that they are wrong. Wrong, from Hopkins's point
of view (he disliked the 'enervating qualities' in Keats),
and in the light of a whole literature which has offered
personal truthfulness to decorative grace in art. Against
Keats's 'Beauty is Truth, Truth Beauty,' we might
set Renard's 'La vérité n'est pas toujours l'art, l'art
n'est pas toujours la vérité, mais la vérité et l'art
ont des points de contact; je les cherche'. The aim, in
fact, of an artist should be, not to create as beautifully
as possible, but to tell as much of the truth as is
compatible with creating beautifully. One result of
this will be the creation of a far more personal and
precise literature, a littérature contre la littérature,
in which fancy, no longer plays a dominant part. .

plane. This definition must vary as the plane varies, an exquisite plane being merely illustrative.[1]

38. It would be truer to say that Chinese painting is a branch of poetry and that calligraphy is the medium of both[.]

W. B. Honey, The Eumorfopoulos Collection Apollo, Oct. 1936, p. 204[2]

39. ". . [.] we see his false start as a poet reaching its climax in Heaven-Haven[3] (1866). . [. .] The point about Heaven-Haven[4] and all his poems of that kind is not so much that they are bad—some indeed are exquisite—as that they are wrong.[5] Wrong from Hopkins's point of view (he disliked the 'enervating qualities' in Keats), and in the light of a whole literature which has opposed personal truthfulness to decorative grace in art. Against Keats's 'Beauty is Truth, Truth Beauty', we[6] might set Renard's '*La vérité n'est pas toujours l'art; l'art n'est pas toujours la vérité, mais la vérité et l'art ont des points de contact; je les cherche*'.[7] The aim, in fact, of an artist should be, not to create as beautifully as possible, but to tell as much of the truth as is compatible with creating beautifully. One result of this will be the creation of a far more personal and precise literature, a *littérature contre la littérature*,[8] in which fancy no longer plays a dominant part. . [. .]

Quichotte (Paris: La Renaissance du Livre, 1922) and *Journal et Voyages* (Paris: Le Divan, 1934), both sold at auction on 10 Mar. 1959 by Parke-Bernet Galleries.

[7] Source: [. . .] *contemporary*

[8] Source: will yet be

[9] Sic, for Schoenberg

[10] David Joseph Bach, "A Note on Arnold Schoenberg," *Musical Quarterly*, 22 (Jan. 1936), 10-11.

---

[1] Also included in *OP* 180 and Litz, p. 67. Speaking of pure poetry in "The Irrational Element in Poetry," a lecture delivered at Harvard in December 1936, Stevens asked, "When we find in poetry that which gives us a momentary existence on an exquisite plane, is it necessary to ask the meaning of the poem?" (*OP* 223).

[2] W. B. Honey, "The Eumorfopoulos Collection: III.—Paintings & Sculpture," *Apollo*, 24 (Oct. 1936), 204.

[3] Source: *Heaven-Haven*

In "Notes toward a Supreme Fiction" (1942), Stevens imagines a moment "when the moon hangs on the wall / Of heaven-haven" (*CP* 398-99).

[4] Source: *Heaven-Haven*

[5] Source: *wrong.*

[6] Source: Beauty" we

[7] Not italicized in source. "Truth is not always art; art is not always truth, but truth and art have points of contact; I look for them."

[8] "literature opposed to literature"

It needs more imagination to see and interpret the
world as it is "
                    The New Statesman And Nation, Jan.
                    23, 1937, p.124, The Young Hopkins
                    by G. W. Stonier

Cézanne at the Lefèvre.
        "But these .. qualities (of 'varied and inimitable'
colour and his handling) .. do not account for the
look of hard and unrelenting authenticity, that
distinguishes his work from that of lesser men. It
is Cézanne's peculiar determination to pin down his
sensation, and the exactness and intensity of notation
resulting from this, that made Cézanne pre-eminent.
.. In a Cézanne there can be no question of juggling
with the elements of design, no possibility of glossing
over difficulties, no equivocation. With Cézanne integrity was the thing, and integrity never allowed
him to become fixed at any one point in his
development, but sent him onward toward new
discoveries of technique, new realisations of the
motif."
                    The New Statesman and Nation, June
                    12, 1937, p.963 by Graham Bell
I note the above both for itself and because it adds
to subject and manner the thing that is incessantly overlooked: the artist, the presence of the
determining personality. Without that vanity, no

It needs more imagination to see and interpret the world as it is[.]"
    The New Statesman And Nation, Jan. 23, 1937, p. 124. The Young
Hopkins by G. W. Stonier[1]

40. *Cézanne at the Lefèvre.*
    "But these . . [.] qualities (of 'varied and inimitable' colour and his han-
dling) . . [.] do not account for the look of hard and unrelenting authenticity that distinguishes his work from that of lesser men. It is Cézanne's
peculiar determination to pin down his sensation, and the exactness and
intensity of notation resulting from this, that made[2] Cézanne pre-
eminent. . . [.] In a Cézanne there can be no question of juggling with
the elements of design, no possibility of glossing over difficulties, no
equivocation. With Cézanne integrity was the thing, and integrity never
allowed him to become fixed at any one point in his development, but
sent him onward toward new discoveries of technique, new realisations
of the motive."
    The New Statesman And Nation, June 12, 1937, p. 963 by Graham Bell[3]
I note the above both for itself and because it adds to subject and manner
the thing that is incessantly overlooked: the artist, the presence of the
determining personality. Without that reality no

[1] G. W. Stonier, "The Young Hopkins," rev. of *The Note-Books and Papers of Gerard Manley Hopkins*, ed. Humphry House, *New Statesman and Nation*, 23 Jan. 1937, pp. 124, 126.
    [2] Source: make
    [3] Graham Bell, "No Equivocation: Cézanne, at the Lefèvre," *New Statesman and Nation*, 12 June 1937, p. 963.

amount of other things matters much.

From Correspondance de Jules Renard

"... je tâche, en restant exact, d'être poète"

p. 224   A Louis Paillard 1er Sept. 1900

"Quoi de plus moral qu'un grand poète?"

p. 277   A Isidore Gaujour 13 Mars 1903

An objection to originality in poetry is an objection
to poetry itself because originality is of the essence
of the thing. Renard wrote to Rostand that one of
his books was "jeune, surprenant, émouvant et joli".
The original is the surprenant, even the émouvant.

Of phrases: ("poissons avec des couleurs de parade
qui viennent se heurter à la page"):
    "Le monde des poissons est une fête sans
joie; il raut nos yeux en laissant notre coeur
dans l'indifférence."
        A Abel Bonnard: Le monde des poissons.

"Ce n'est point une nécessité qu'il y ait du sang
et des morts dans une tragédie: il suffit que
l'action en soit grande, que les acteurs en soient
héroïques, que les passions y soient excitées et que
ressente de cette tristesse majestueuse qui fait
tout le plaisir de la tragédie. .(Then follows
a precept respecting simplicity, as to which) il

ressentir : porter le
caractère de

[1937]

amount of other things matters much.[1]

41. From Correspondance de Jules Renard[2]
     ". . [.] je tâche, en restant exact, d'être poëte[.]"[3]
       p. 224 À Louis Paillard 1ᵉ Sept. 1900[4]
     "Quoi de plus moral qu'un grand poête?"[5]
       p. 277 À Isidore Gaujour 13 Mars 1903[6]

42. An objection to originality in poetry is an objection to poetry itself be-
    cause originality is of the essence of the thing. Renard wrote to Rostand[7]
    that one of his books was "jeune, surprenant, emouvant[8] et joli".[9] The
    original is the surprenant, even the emouvant.

43. Of phrases etc ("poissons avec des couleurs de parade, qui viennent se
    heurter à la page"[10]):
      "Le monde des poissons est une fête sans joie; il ravit nos yeux en lais-
    sant notre coeur dans l'indifférence."[11]
      Abel Bonnard: Le Monde des poissons.[12]

44. "Ce n'est point une nécessité qu'il y ait du sang et des morts dans une
    tragédie: il suffit que l'action en soit grande, que les acteurs en soient
    héroïques, que les passions y soient excitées et que ressente[13] de cette
    tristesse majestueuse qui fait tout le plaisir de la tragédie. . [. .] (Then fol-
    lows a precept respecting simplicity as to which) il

[1] Included in *OP* xxxix.
[2] The page numbers cited by Stevens correspond to those in the *Correspondance de Jules Renard* (Paris: François Bernouard, 1928); this is the source cited in subsequent notes to the entry.
[3] ". . . I try, by remaining accurate, to be a poet." George Lensing notes (p. 217) that Stevens
used this excerpt, with minor changes, as the epigraph of "United Dames of America"
(1937, *CP* 206).
[4] Source: A Louis Paillard [. . .] 1ᵉʳ *septembre* 1900.
[5] Source: grand poëte? "What is more moral than a great poet?"
[6] Source: A Isidore Gaujour [. . .] 13 *mars* 1903.
[7] *Correspondance* (see Entry 41), p. 164.
[8] Source: émouvant
[9] "youthful, surprising, moving, and lovely." Edmond Rostand's *La Samaritaine* is the book
so described.
[10] "fish of gaudy colors, that collide against the page." I cannot find these words in *Le Monde des
poissons*; Stevens may have taken them, and possibly also the excerpt that follows, from a review
of the book.
[11] "The world of fish is a festival without joy; it delights our eyes while leaving our heart
indifferent."
[12] Abel Bonnard, *Le Monde des poissons* (Paris: Librairie Plon, 1937), p. 5.
[13] In Paul Mesnard's edition of the *Oeuvres de J. Racine*, II (Paris: Hachette, 1865), this passage
from the preface to *Bérénice* reads, "excitées, et que tout s'y ressente" (p. 366). In the margin to
the left of the word *ressente*, Stevens has written: ressentir: porter le caractère de.

ne faut point croire que cette règle ne soit fondée que sur
la fantaisie de ceux qui l'ont faite. Il n'y a que le vraisemblable qui touche dans la tragédie".

        Racine, Préface, Bérénice, 1670.

Racine, too, was a tea drinker
        Edward Bunyard, The Epicure's Companion p345

"The aim of the serious dramatist is to invent a situation in which several characters reveal – in a way
which is spontaneous because it is produced by the
situation – the fundamental nature of their being
and their attitude to life. Now the poet is someone
who devotes his life to exactly such a process of
self-revelation as drama attempts to produce in
characters: his poems are speeches from the drama
of the time in which he's living. The dramatist defines in his characters the level at which their
feelings blend into poetry".

        Stephen Spender, Poetry And Expression-
ism. New Statesman & Nation, March 16, 1978

"It is less difficult for the philosopher than
for the artist to be in disagreement with his period.
There is little parallel between the two cases. The
one pours his spirit into a creative work, the other
ponders on the real with the understanding
mind. It is in the first case by depending

ne faut point croire que cette règle ne soit fondée que sur la fantaisie de ceux qui l'ont faite. Il n'y a que le vraisemblable qui touche dans la tragédie".[1]

Racine, Préface, Bérénice, 1670.

45. Racine, too, was a tea drinker[2]
Edward Bunyard, The Epicure's Companion p 345[3]

46. "The aim of the serious dramatist is to invent a situation in which several characters reveal—in a way which is spontaneous because it is produced by the situation—the fundamental nature of their being and their attitude to life. Now the poet is someone who devotes his life to exactly such a process of self-revelation as drama attempts to produce in characters: his poems are speeches from the drama of the time in which he is living.[4] The dramatist defines in his characters the level at which their feelings blend into poetry".

Stephen Spender, Poetry And Expressionism, New Statesman & Nation, March 12, 1938[5]

47. "It is less difficult for the philosopher than for the artist to be in disagreement with his period. There is little parallel between the two cases. The one pours his spirit into a creative work, the other ponders on the real with the understanding mind. It is in the first case by depending

---

[1] "There is no need whatsoever for blood and corpses in a tragedy: it suffices that its action be grand, that its characters be heroic, that the passions be roused in it, and that everything in it bear the mark of that majestic sadness which constitutes all the pleasure of tragedy. . . . [O]ne must not think that that rule is founded solely on the whimsy of those who made it up. Only the probable is moving in tragedy."

Writing to Latimer on 23 Dec. 1937, Stevens said, "Recently, Racine (who understood so perfectly the same sort of people that you and I have so much difficulty in understanding) has had an immense attraction for me" (letter in the Ronald Lane Latimer Papers, University of Chicago Library).

[2] Source: drinker, and it would seem an ideal drink for the taut style he carried to its perfection.

[3] Edward and Lorna Bunyard, *The Epicure's Companion* (London: J. M. Dent, 1937), p. 345.

[4] Stevens could be recalling this passage in his poem "Of Modern Poetry" (1940):

[Poetry] has to be living, to learn the speech of the place.
It has to face the men of the time and to meet
The women of the time. It has to think about war
And it has to find what will suffice. It has
To construct a new stage. It has to be on that stage
And, like an insatiable actor, slowly and
With meditation, speak words that in the ear,
In the delicatest ear of the mind, repeat,
Exactly, that which it wants to hear. . . . (CP 240)

[5] Stephen Spender, "Poetry and Expressionism," *New Statesman and Nation*, 12 Mar. 1938, pp. 407-8.

on the intellect of his time and pressing it to
the limit, in the concentration of all his energies
and all his fire, that the artist has a chance
of reshaping the whole mass"

       Jacques Maritain, The Degrees of
       Knowledge p. 4 of the Introduction:
       The Grandeur And Misery Of Metaphysics

"This scalic freedom of line and mastery of ellipsis is the secret of all his harmonic complexity, the unique aristocratic tang . . . his writing
is 'technically' strict, and his harmonic dialect
rooted in the practice of his forbears, yet, by
means of these elliptical transitions and flexible basses, he can produce chordal sequences
which are absolutely original and inimitable,
though containing no chord which is extraordinary
in itself . . Bach himself, sometimes but not often-
in the Chromatic Fantasia and Fugue for instance-
achieved, by means of his exploitation of chromaticism, a comparable quince-like subtlety.
You can sense it . . as perhaps the most delicate
flower of human culture"

       The Composer And 'Civilization', Notes On
       The Later Work Of Gabriel Fauré, by W.
       H. Mellers in Scrutiny for March, 1938, p.395.

Mellers quotes Fauré as saying,

on the intellect of his time and pressing it to the limit, in the concentration of all his languor and all his fire, that the artist has a chance of reshaping the whole mass[.]"

Jacques Maritain, The Degrees of Knowledge p 4 of the Introduction: The Grandeur And Misery Of Metaphysics.[1]

48. "This scalic freedom of line and mastery of ellipsis is the secret of all his harmonic complexity, the unique aristocratic tang. . . [.] his writing is 'technically' strict, and his harmonic dialect rooted in the practice of his forbears, yet, by means of these elliptical transitions and flexible basses, he can produce chordal sequences which are absolutely original and inimitable, though containing no chord which is extraordinary in itself. . [. .] Bach himself, sometimes but not often—in the *Chromatic Fantasia and Fugue* for instance—achieved, by means of his exploitation of chromaticism, a comparable quince-like subtlety. You can sense it . . [.] as perhaps the most delicate flower of humane culture[.]"

The Composer And 'Civilization', Notes On The Later Work Of Gabriel Fauré, by W. H. Mellers in Scrutiny for March, 1938, p. 395.[2]

Mellers quotes Fauré as saying,

[1] Jacques Maritain, *The Degrees of Knowledge*, trans. Bernard Wall and Margot R. Adamson (London: G. Bles, Centenary Press, 1937), p. 4.

[2] W. H. Mellers, "The Composer and 'Civilization': Notes on the Later Work of Gabriel Fauré," *Scrutiny*, 6 (Mar. 1938), 395. Michael Stegman lists six Fauré phonograph records in his discography, pp. 87-88.

"L'artiste doit aimer la vie et nous montrer
qu'elle est belle. Sans lui, nous en douterions"

"A renascence of poetry in painting would be
altogether welcome, but the mythology of 'malleable
watches' and 'drawers of flesh' invented by
M. Dali is inadequately imaginative. H is
paranoia is altogether too deliberate. 'N'est
pas fou qui voudrait !' "
New Statesman and Nation June 27, 1938 /2, 1029

"Certes" writes M. François Mauriac in a
preface to a first novel, Les Enfants aveugles, by
a young novelist, M. Bruno Gay-Lussac,
"je m'attends à des reproches." The novel is
not "edifiante". 'Hé quoi ! c'est là tout ce qu'un
académicien catholique trouve à porter
aux nues .... La vertu essentielle de l'é-
crivain réside, à nos yeux, dans une certaine attitude devant le réel, faite d'honnêteté, de scrupule et de candeur, dans
l'acharnement à creuser le roc d'un être
jusqu'à la nappe d'eau, jusqu'à la
source profonde."

A just pleasing of Picasso:
"Picasso, unfortunately, has made his name
pre-eminently as an intellectualist; a man, that is,

"L'artiste doit aimer la vie et nous montrer qu'elle est belle. Sans lui, nous en douterions[.]"[1]

49. "A renascence of poetry in painting would be altogether welcome, but the mythology of 'malleable watches' and 'drawers of flesh' invented by M. Dali is inadequately imaginative. His paranoia is altogether too deliberate.[2] 'N'est pas fou qui voudrait.'"[3]
   New Statesman and Nation June 27, 1938 p. 1029[4]

50. "Certes" writes M. François Mauriac in a preface to a first novel, Les Enfants aveugles, by a young novelist, M. Bruno Gay-Lussac,[5] "je m'attends à des reproches." The novel is not "edifiante".[6] "[']Hé quoi![7] c'est là tout ce qu'un académicien catholique trouve à porter aux nues. . . [.'] La vertu[8] essentielle de l'écrivain réside, à nos yeux, dans[9] une certaine attitude devant le réel, faite d'honnêteté, de scrupule et de candeur, dans l'acharnement à creuser le roc d'un être jusqu'à la nappe d'eau, jusqu'à la source profonde."[10]

51. A just placing of Picasso:
   "Picasso, unfortunately, has made his name pre-eminently as an intellectualist; a man, that is,

---

[1] Italicized in source, p. 401. "The artist ought to love life and show us that it is beautiful. Without him, we would doubt it."

[2] Source: deliberate:

[3] "No one can will to be mad." That Stevens shared this opinion of Dali and the Surrealists is suggested by one of his adages ("The essential fault of surrealism is that it invents without discovering" [OP 177]), his remark about the "charlatans of the irrational" in "The Irrational Element in Poetry" (1936, OP 228), and a letter to Latimer of 30 Dec. 1936 (L 315).

[4] "Salvador Dali at the Lefèvre," New Statesman and Nation, 27 June 1936, p. 1029. Stevens apparently excerpted this passage in 1938, which would account for the error in the date.

[5] Bruno Gay-Lussac, Les Enfants aveugles (Paris: B. Grasset, 1938). Mauriac's comments appear on p. 8 of the preface.

[6] Sic, for "édifiant." Stevens is paraphrasing Mauriac, who says that for some readers the book "n'offre rien dont le lecteur se puisse dire édifié."

[7] The edition cited above reads: des reproches: "Eh quoi?

[8] The edition cited above reads: aux nues! [. . .]" [. . .] la vertu

[9] The edition cited above reads: réside à nos yeux dans

[10] "To be sure," writes M. François Mauriac . . . , "I expect some criticism." The novel is not "edifying." " 'What of it! That's all a Catholic academician finds to praise to the skies. . . .' . . . [T]he essential virtue of the writer resides, in our eyes, in a certain attitude toward the real, made up of honesty, scrupulousness, and candor, in the keen determination to bore through the bedrock of an individual down to water level, down to the deep springs."

who has not hitherto allowed sentiment to sway him in
his ways. His earliest work was, it is true, sentimental,
but his fame rests entirely on his cool and calculated
exploitation of the elements of formal design, with
or without psychological associations. 'Away from
Nature!' was his slogan. Much of his work — eschewing nature and, therefore, lacking a common
denominator between him and the public — remained,
except as a matter of abstract designing, unintelligible.
Nevertheless, there has appeared in his œuvre abstract form, solidly modelled, that had a grim
significance of human emotions. Perhaps, then, these
things were not as 'mad' as they looked... The
long and short of it is that Picasso is not a painter,
and we have only here and there a detail in the numerous studies, such as a horse's outstretched body, as an
earnest that he is a magnificent draughtsman.
For the rest, he is an over-intellectual designer,
who moves one to thought, but not to feeling."

A note in Apollo for November, 1938,
at p. 266 on Picasso's "Guernica", exhibited
at the New Burlington Galleries in London.

Mais le vrai prodige ne se fabrique pas.
        Marianne Magazine no. 5
This is the same thing as that there is no such
thing as an artificial marvel.

who has not hitherto allowed sentiment to stand in his way. His earliest
work was, it is true, sentimental; but his fame rests entirely on his cool
and calculated exploitation of the elements of formal design, with or
without psychological associations. Away from Nature! was his slogan.
Much of his work—eschewing nature and, therefore, lacking a common
denominator between him and the public—remained, except as a matter
of abstract designing, unintelligible. Nevertheless, there has appeared in
his oeuvre[1] abstract form, solidly modelled, that had a grim significance of
human emotions. Perhaps, then, these things were not as 'mad' as they
looked. . . [.] The long and short[2] of it is that Picasso is not a painter, and
we have only here and there a detail in the numerous studies, such as a
horse's contorted body, as an earnest that he is a magnificent draughtsman. For the rest, he is an over-intellectual designer who moves one to
thought, but not to feeling[.]"

A note in *Apollo* for November, 1938, at p. 266 on Picasso's
"Guernica", exhibited at the New Burlington Galleries in London.[3]

52. Mais le vrai prodige ne se fabrique pas.[4]
Marianne Magazine No. 5[5]
This is the same thing as that there is no such thing as an artificial marvel.

---

[1] Source: *oeuvre*

[2] Source: and the short

[3] [Herbert Furst,] "Picasso's 'Guernica,'" *Apollo*, 28 (Nov. 1938), 266.

[4] "But the true marvel is not manufactured."

[5] I have been unable to find this passage in the fifth number of *Marianne*, dated 23 Nov. 1932, or
in the issues for 1938-1939.

In a perfect community where no one suffers
or is afraid, there are no great voices crying
out for the pity of things.

Life of Letters To-Day, March
1939, Winifred Holmes

But this is often true of a community where
many suffer and many or all are afraid.

"At last, a true musician! He composes in
C natural and no one else but the Almighty
could do that."

Gounod of Charpentier. The musical
Quarterly, July, 1939, p. 337

53. In a perfect community where no one suffers or is afraid, there are no great voices crying out for the pity of things.

     Life & Letters ToDay, March 1939, Winifred Holmes[1]

     But this is often true of a community where many suffer and many or all are afraid.

54. "At last, a true musician! He composes in C natural[2] and no one else but the Almighty could do that."[3]

     Gounod of Charpentier, The Musical Quarterly, July, 1939, p. 337[4]

[1] Winifred Holmes, "Denmark, 1939," *Life and Letters To-Day*, 21 (Mar. 1939), 26.

[2] Source: natural,

[3] Source: that!" Stevens quotes Gounod's remark in a letter to Allen Tate, 18 Oct. 1941 (*L* 393). Among the titles in Stevens' notebook *From Pieces of Paper* is "A Few Pages in C Major" (Lensing, p. 183).

[4] Kathleen O'Donnell Hoover, "Gustave Charpentier," *Musical Quarterly*, 25 (July 1939), 337.

06 journaux

On écrit de telles choses pour transmettre aux autres la
théorie de l'univers qu'on porte en soi. Renan, *Souvenirs*, p. iii

55. Of journals

On écrit de telles choses pour transmettre aux autres la théorie de l'univers qu'on porte en soi.[1] Renan, Souvenirs, p. iii[2]

[1] "One writes about such things to communicate to others the theory of the universe one harbors in oneself."

[2] This entry is taken from p. 163 of *Walter Leaf 1852-1927*, which suggests that Stevens entered it in his commonplace book at the same time as Entry 5. In *Walter Leaf* the citation of Ernest Renan occupies a separate line; Renan's words and *Souvenirs* are in italic type.

Cahier II

SUR PLUSIEURS

BEAUX

SUJECTS

II

Of humanism, heroes...

"I need badly to find one man in history to admire. I am in near peril of turning Christian, and rolling in the mud in the agony of human mortification."

Henry Adams in a letter, Feb. 15, 1915, to Henry Osborn Taylor, quoted in The Kenyon Review, Winter, 1940.

"To most of us great art is terrifying till it has been sterilised by age and usage and some years of confinement in a museum. Only then does that explosive assertion of a temperament, which is what live art must be, become familiar and acceptable to the public . . 'Ultra-modern art' is art untamed."

Clive Bell, New Statesman, Jan. 6, 1940.

La vie ne laisse plus guère de place ni à la fantaisie ni aux traditions, qui lui donnaient saveur et couleur.

"Finally, Alexander's philosophy is Victorian in its optimism. The nature of the universe is, it appears, that of a progress. Space is the raw material of things; time is its mind; at a particular stage of the progress life emerges; at the end deity is reached. The universe

56. Of humanism, heroes . . .

  "I need badly to find one man in history to admire. I am in near peril of turning Christian, and rolling in the mud in the agony[1] of human mortification[.]"[2]

  Henry Adams in a letter, Feb. 15, 1915, to Henry Osborn Taylor, quoted in The Kenyon Review, Winter, 1940.[3]

57. "To most of us great art is terrifying till it has been sterilised by age and usage and some years of confinement in a museum. Only then does that explosive assertion of a temperament, which is what live art must be, become familiar and acceptable to the public. . [. .] 'Ultra-modern art' is art untamed."

  Clive Bell, New Statesman, Jan. 6, 1940[4]

58. La vie ne laisse plus guere[5] de place ni à la fantaisie ni aux traditions, qui lui donnaient saveur et couleur.[6]

— —

59. "Finally, Alexander's philosophy is Victorian in its optimism. The nature of the universe is, it appears, that of a progress. Space is the raw material of things; time is its[7] mind; at a particular stage of the progress life emerges; at the end deity is reached. The universe

---

[1] Source: an agony

[2] Stevens would echo Adams' sentiment in a letter to Henry Church of 20 Nov. 1945, where he speaks of his need to encounter "the well developed individual, the master of life, or the man who by his mere appearance convinces you that a mastery of life is possible" (L 518).

[3] R. P. Blackmur, "Henry Adams: Three Late Moments," *Kenyon Review*, 2 (Winter 1940), 26. Stevens' "Variations on a Summer Day" appeared in this issue.

[4] Clive Bell, "Mr. Munnings and Ultra-Modern Art," *New Statesman and Nation*, 6 Jan. 1940, p. 11.

[5] Sic, for guère

[6] "Life no longer leaves much room for imagination or traditions, which used to give it savor and color." Stevens also entered this quotation (whose source is unknown) in his notebook *From Pieces of Paper*; see Lensing, p. 167. In his lecture "The Noble Rider and the Sound of Words" (1941), Stevens maintains that the poet "has had immensely to do with giving life whatever savor it possesses" (*NA* 30).

[7] Source: time its

in fact is a striving towards deity which
succeeds. God did not make the world, but
the world evolves into God. Possibly, possibly
not! Fifty years ago, the nature of things did
look as if it were going to the good rather than
to the devil."

    C.E.M. Joad   New Statesman, March
    2, 1940 : of Samuel Alexander, O.M.
    (Space, Time And Deity, 1920)

.. the human will, taken either in the individual or in society as a whole, is the principle of evil.

    William Troy : On Rereading Balzac
    Kenyon Review II, 3 . p. 334

The Incamminati of Bologna led by the
Carracci cousins, Lodovico, Agostino and Annibale, who sought to achieve perfection by the
practice of an addition sum of qualities .. Add
the drawing of the Roman School to the movement
and chiaroscuro of the Venetian, the terribilità
of Michelangelo, the naturalism of Titian, the
balance of Raphael and the grace of Correggio
and Parmigiano and the greatest art must
result

    (no note of the source of this)

in fact is a striving towards deity *which succeeds*. God did not make the world, but the world evolves into God. Possibly, possibly not! Fifty years ago, the nature of things did look as if it were going to the good rather than to the devil."

    C. E. M. Joad New Statesman, March 2, 1940: of Samuel Alexander, O. M. (Space, Time And Deity, 1920)[1]

60. . . . [.] the human will, taken either in the individual or in society as a whole, is the principle of evil.
    William Troy: On Rereading Balzac
    Kenyon Review II, 3, p. 334[2]

61. The Incamminati[3] of Bologna led by the Carracci cousins, Ludovico, Agostino and Annibale, who sought to achieve perfection by the practice of an addition sum of qualities . . [.] Add the drawing of the Roman School to the movement and chiaroscuro[4] of the Venetian,[5] the terribilita[6] of Michelangelo, the naturalism of Titian, the balance of Raphael and the grace of Correggio and Parmigiano[7] and the greatest art must result[.]
    (No note of the source of this)[8]

---

[1] C. E. M. Joad, "Another Great Victorian," rev. of *Philosophical and Literary Pieces*, by Samuel Alexander, *New Statesman and Nation*, 2 Mar. 1940, p. 282. Stevens quotes Alexander's *Space, Time and Deity* in "A Collect of Philosophy" (1951, *OP* 193-94).

[2] William Troy, "On Rereading Balzac: The Artist as Scapegoat," *Kenyon Review*, 2 (Summer 1940), 334.

[3] Source: There were, for example, the Incamminati

[4] Source: *chiaroscuro*

[5] Source: Venetians,

[6] Source: *terribilita*

[7] Source: and of Parmigiano

[8] Stevens' source is Herbert Furst, "How to Appreciate Art, Part X—Prejudice," *Apollo*, 32 (Aug. 1940), 45.

Civilization is the process of reducing the infinite to the finite.

O. W. H. to Sir F. P.

II Holmes-Pollock Letters 104

Yet when one suspects that a man knows something about life that one hasn't heard before one is uneasy until one has found out what he has to say.

do. 139

ILLA CANTAT; NOS TACEAMUS. QUANDO VERVENIT MEUM?
QUANDO FACIAM UT CHELIDON UT TACERE DESINAM?
PERDIDI MUSAM TACENDO; NEC ME PHOEBUS RESPICIT
PERVIGILIUM

Pasternak declared that the artist must expect no other aid than from his own imagination, that art should represent the furthest reach and not the mean of an epoch, and that the natural growth and strength of art can relate it to its period . . the first essential condition for the creation of works of art is that the artist must be allowed freely to follow his own imagination — whether it may lead him into the front line or, more often, into isolation. Art is individual and the artist, therefore, is an individualist so no demands can be made on him from the outside.

62. Civilization is the process of reducing the infinite to the finite.
     O. W. H. to Sir F. P.
     II Holmes-Pollock Letters 104[1]
Yet when one suspects that a man[2] knows something about life that one hasn't heard before one is uneasy until one has found out what he has to say.
     do. 139[3]

63. ILLA CANTAT; NOS TACEMUS. QUANDO VER VENIT MEUM?
    QUANDO FACIAM UT CHELIDON UT TACERE DESINAM?
    PERDIDI MUSAM TACENDO; NEC ME PHOEBUS RESPICIT [.][4]

                    PERVIGILIUM[5]

64. Pasternak declared that the artist must expect no other aid than from his own imagination, that art should represent the furthest reach and not the mean of an epoch, and that the natural growth and strength of art can relate it to its period. . [. .] the first essential condition for the creation of works of art is that the artist must be allowed freely to follow his own imagination—whether it may lead him into the front-line or, more often, into isolation. Art is individual and the artist, therefore, is an individualist and no demands can be made on him from the outside.

---

[1] *Holmes-Pollock Letters: The Correspondence of Mr. Justice Holmes and Sir Frederick Pollock, 1874-1932*, ed. Mark DeWolfe Howe (Cambridge, Mass.: Harvard Univ. Press, 1941), II, 104; the following excerpt is from the same volume, p. 139.

[2] Oswald Spengler, whose *Der Untergang des Abendlandes* Holmes had been reading.

[3] The abbreviation preceding the page number appears to be "do."—probably for "ditto."

[4] "She sings; we remain quiet. When does my springtime come?
   When shall I be like the swallow, that I may cease to be silent?
   I have lost the Muse by keeping still; nor does Phoebus look my way."

[5] This passage, part of which Eliot uses in *The Waste Land*, is from the final stanza of the *Pervigilium Veneris*. In a letter to Allen Tate of 3 Jan. 1944, thanking Tate for a copy of his translation of the *Pervigilium*, Stevens mentions that he had "three or four" other translations at home (*L* 460). These were apparently among the books Elsie sold to a bookseller around 1958, as only Tate's *The Vigil of Venus* remains in the extant portion of Stevens' library.

Stefan Schimanski : in *Voice of the*
Younger Writers - *Life & Letters To-Day*,
February, 1943, p. 90 et p. 95.

L'esthétique est une justice supérieure
　　　　　　　　Flaubert

We ought to have discovered by now that all
ages are in reality a complex of conflicting
ideas on every subject and the products of the
age are just what they are because of the conflict, not because of general agreement.
　　　　George Boas in *Gazette des Beaux-
Arts*, June, 1943, p. 381

Je vis de bonne soupe et pas de beau langage.
　　　Paul Bonifas to Philaminte in
　　　　　　Les Femmes Savantes

It is art which makes life, makes interest, makes
importance .. and I know of no substitute whatever
for the force and beauty of its process.
　　　　　　Henry James

[.. the radical crisis of Italian society] its nature
can be plainly described by saying that there
.. a small minority .. was living .. rearing
intellectual structures .. without any real
connection with and without any real care

[1943-1944]

Stefan Schimanski: The Duty of the Younger Writer, Life & Letters To-Day, February, 1943, p. 90 at p. 95.[1]

65. L'esthétique est une justice supérieure[.][2]
    Flaubert

66. We ought to have discovered by now that all ages are in reality a complex of conflicting ideas on every subject and the products of the age are just what they are because of the conflict, not because of general agreement.
    George Boas in Gazette des Beaux-Arts, June, 1943, p. 381[3]

67. Je vis de bonne soupe et pas de beau language.[4]
    Paul Bonifas to Philaminte in Les Femmes Savantes[5]

68. It is art which makes life,[6] makes interest, makes importance . . [.] and I know of no substitute whatever for the force and beauty of its process.
    Henry James[7]

69. [[. . [.] the radical crisis of Italian society]] Its nature can be plainly described by saying that there . . [.] a small minority . . [.] was living[, .] . . rearing intellectual structures . . [.] without any real connection with and without any real care

---

[1] Stefan Schimanski, "The Duty of the Younger Writer," *Life and Letters To-Day*, 36 (Feb. 1943), 95-96.

[2] This paraphrases a sentence in Flaubert's letter to George Sand of "Thursday night" (sometime in October 1871): "Bref, la première injustice est pratiquée par la littérature qui n'a souci de l'esthétique, laquelle n'est qu'une Justice supérieure" ("In short, the chief injustice is practiced by literature that doesn't bother about aesthetic, which is precisely a higher Justice"). The sentence can be found in the *Oeuvres complètes de Gustave Flaubert: Correspondance*, VI (Paris: Louis Conard, 1930), 296. Stevens' twenty-one volume set of this edition is now at the Huntington Library.

[3] George Boas, rev. of *Art and Freedom*, by Horace M. Kallen, *Gazette des Beaux-Arts*, 23 (June 1943), 381.

[4] language: sic, for langage. Most editions of Molière's play read, "Je vis de bonne soupe, et non de beau langage" ("I live on good soup and not on beautiful language").
    Speaking in "The Relations between Poetry and Painting" (1951) of trendy typographic experiments in modern poetry, Stevens says, "They have nothing to do with the conflict between the poet and that of which his poems are made. They are neither 'bonne soupe' nor 'beau langage'" (*NA* 168).

[5] Actually, Chrysale is speaking to Philaminte and Bélise (*Les Femmes savantes*, II.vii.531).

[6] In Percy Lubbock's edition of *The Letters of Henry James* (New York: Scribners, 1920), II, 490, the first part of the sentence reads: It is art that *makes* life, etc.

[7] Stevens quotes this passage, taken from James's letter to H. G. Wells of 10 July 1915, in "The Relations between Poetry and Painting" (*NA* 169).

for the life, the toil, the feelings and the mentality
of the enormous majority of their fellow men;
actually without any real care for each other.
And there, in that compact and dumb ignorance
were the roots of their frightful unreality.

Nicola Chiaromonte : Croce and
Italian Liberalism . Politics (Sept. 1944) 136

I followed his argument with the blank uneasiness
which one might feel in the presence of a logical
lunatic.

Victor Serge : The Revolution At Dead-
End . Politics (June. 1944) 150

"As early as 1275 Giraud Riquier declared that 'it
is God who wills to honour poets not to be got from
any other man. In all other branches of learning
good teaching is precious, but if God does not endow a man at the outset with knowledge of
poetry he will never gain it.' "

E. E. Kellett in a review of "From Script
to Print" by H. J. Chaytor in The New Statesman
and Nation March 3, 1945 (p. 145)

I do set my bow in the cloud and it shall be
for a token of a covenant between me and the
earth.

Gen. IX : 13

for the life, the toil, the feelings and the mentality of the enormous majority of their fellow men; actually without[1] any real care for each other. And
there, in that compact and dumb ignorance, were the roots of their frightful unreality.

Nicola Chiaromonte: Croce and Italian Liberalism, Politics (June
1944) 136[2]

70. I followed his argument with the blank uneasiness which one might feel
in the presence of a logical lunatic.

Victor Serge: The Revolution At Dead-End, Politics (June, 1944), 150[3]

71. "As early as 1275 Giraud Riquier declared that 'it is God who wills to
honour poets not to be got[4] from any other man. In all other branches of
learning good teaching is precious, but if God does not endow a man at
the outset with knowledge of poetry he will never gain it.'"

E. E. Kellett in a review of "From Script to Print" by H. J. Chaytor in
The New Statesman and Nation March 3, 1945 (p. 145.)[5]

72. I do set my bow in the cloud and it shall be for a token of a covenant
between me and the earth.

Gen. IX: 13

[1] Source: actually, without

[2] Nicola Chiaromonte, "Croce and Italian Liberalism," *Politics*, 1 (June 1944), 136.

[3] Victor Serge, "The Revolution at Dead-End (1926-1928)," trans. Ethel Libson, *Politics*, 1 (June
1944), 150. Stevens quotes Serge verbatim in "Esthétique du Mal," XIV (1944, *CP* 324). Serge, a
member of the Left Opposition who was later exiled from Russia, here recalls his meeting in 1920
with Konstantinov, an examining magistrate for the Cheka. For further background and discussion, see D. L. Macdonald, "Wallace Stevens and Victor Serge," *Dalhousie Review*, 66 (Spring and
Summer 1986), 174-80.

[4] Source: to honour poets with knowledge not to be got

[5] E. E. Kellett, "Medieval Literature," rev. of *From Script to Print*, by H. J. Chaytor, *New Statesman and Nation*, 3 Mar. 1945, p. 145.

"To live in the world of creation — to get into it
and stay in it — to frequent it and haunt it —
to think intensely and fruitfully — to woo combinations and inspirations into being by a
depth and continuity of attention and meditation — this is the only thing."

Henry James   New Statesman,
May 26, 1945, — p. 339. A review
of F. O. Matthiesen's H. J.: the
Major Phase.

Life is always insipid to those who have
no great works in hand and no lofty aims
to elevate their feeling.

Horace Bushnell : On an estab-
lation of the Memorial.

Only by labouring under the authority of
ideas, can we be serenely detached and
purely inspired.

James Guthrie : The Book Craftsman, Vol. I, No. 1 1934

At sixty-four Bartók was not old. Torn and
tormented, he was still an avant-gardiste —
in a way the only one of our time. Knowing
his destination, hardly susceptible to success,
and untouched by official or public unawar-

73. ["]To live *in* the world of creation—to get into it and stay in it—to frequent it and haunt it—to *think* intensely and fruitfully—to woo combinations and inspirations into being by a depth and continuity of attention and meditation—this is the only thing[.]"

   Henry James New Statesman, May 26, 1945, p. 339.[1] A notice of F. O. Matthiesen's[2] H. J[.]: the Major Phase.

74. Life is always insipid to those who have no great works in hand and no lofty aims to elevate their feeling.[3]

   Horace Bushnell: On an entablature of the Memorial.

75. Only[4] by labouring under the authority of ideas, can we be serenely detached and purely inspired.

   James Guthrie: The Book Craftsman, Vol. I, No. 1 1934[5]

76. ["]At sixty-four Bartók was not old. Torn and tormented, he was still an *avant-gardiste*—in a way the only one of our time. Knowing his destination, hardly susceptible to success, and untouched by official or public unaware-

---

[1] John Russell, rev. of *Henry James: The Major Phase*, by F. O. Matthiessen, *New Statesman and Nation*, 26 May 1945, p. 339. Stevens quotes this passage in a letter to José Rodríguez Feo of 20 June 1945 (*L* 506). The review may have prompted him to look at Matthiessen's book, for in a subsequent letter to Rodríguez Feo (probably written in early July) he cites *Henry James: The Major Phase*, p. 10, as the source of the quotation. What remains of the letter is reprinted in *Secretaries of the Moon: The Letters of Wallace Stevens and José Rodríguez Feo*, ed. Beverly Coyle and Alan Filreis (Durham: Duke Univ. Press, 1986), pp. 65-66.

[2] Sic, for Matthiessen's

[3] Stevens quotes these words from memory in a postscript to his July 1945 letter to José Rodríguez Feo (see note to Entry 73). He may have decided to check his memory, for apparently on a stroll past Bushnell Memorial Hall he copied the inscription in pencil on a 10" x 13" manila envelope now at the Huntington Library. Then, probably after transferring the quotation to his commonplace book, he partly erased the note on the envelope.

[4] Source: And only

[5] James Guthrie, "The Hand Printer and His Work," *The Book Craftsman*, 1 (Oct. 1934), 4.

ness of his genius, he pursued his course with unerring self-reliance.

A solitary mind, he was not easy to approach. But his friendships were built on rock. He lived the simple life of a scholar, a busy, secluded, almost monotonous life ... He did not understand the little amenities of sociability ... and rejected them with a child-like, brusque, perturbed amazement ... His words were few and to the point; his interests, intense and critical. His judgment was uncompromising in the rejection of all moral, mental, or artistic dishonesty.

Adversities, bitter experiences, or happiness could not change his character. This explains, in the last analysis, the inner logic of his artistic history, the rare consistency of his new and individual style, the unromantic and universality of his emotions. The portrait of the man and his work consists of diametrically opposed features: frailness and energy, critical mind and naiveté, modesty and self-reliance, icy alertness and fiery humanity, accuracy in minutiae and generosity in matters of importance, virgin purity and elemental sensuality, the cool concentration of research and the ravishing fever of creation.

Béla Bartók (1881-1945) by OTTO GOMBOSI, The Musical Quarterly XXX, no1. (Jan. 1946) p. 9

ness of his genius, he pursued his course with unerring self-reliance.

A[1] solitary soul, he was not easy to approach. But his friendships were built on rock. He lived the simple life of a scholar, a busy, secluded, almost monotonous life. . [. .] He did not understand the little amenities of sociability . . [.] and rejected them with a child-like, brusque, perturbed amazement. . [. .] His words were few and to the point; his interests, intense and critical. His judgment was uncompromising in the rejection of all moral, mental, or artistic dishonesty.[2]

Adversities,[3] bitter experiences, or happiness could not change his character. This explains, in the last analysis, the inner logic of his artistic history, the rare consistency of his new and individual style, the unromantic and[4] universality of his emotions. The portrait of the man and his work consists of diametrically opposed features: frailness and energy, critical mind and naiveté, modesty and self-reliance, icy aloofness and fiery humanity, accuracy in minutiae and generosity in matters of importance, virgin purity and elemental sensuality, the cool concentration of research and the ravishing fever of creation[.]"

Béla Bartók (1881-1945) by Otto Gombosi, The Musical Quarterly XXX, No 1, (Jan. 1946) p. 9[5]

---

[1] Source: begins indented paragraph
[2] Source: dishonesty. [. . .]
[3] Source: begins indented paragraph
[4] Source: unromantic intensity and
[5] Otto Gombosi, "Béla Bartók (1881-1945)," *Musical Quarterly*, 32 (Jan. 1946), 9. Michael Stegman's discography lists two Bartók phonograph records, p. 82.

In a note on Le Parfum de Combray, by P. L. Larcher, the New Yorker in one of its numbers for February, 1946, said that it was at Combray that Marcel Proust, when young, was accustomed to visit his uncle Jules Amiot "summers" "until hay fever prevented his further collecting these seasonal souvenirs, a precious if peculiar harvest which seems only chaff to the young, postwar French: These young Maquis intellectuals, disoriented and restless, spurn left-over literature as unreal."

"Naturally, Klee's anarchic ideals and anarchic personality, appeal to that of Herbert Read, whose great contribution to aesthetic thought has been the demand that an artist should have the right to find and pursue his own vision unhammered by traditional art or cross reference to the appearances of nature ... Part of the risks taken by the extreme individualist in art: that he has deliberately departed from common experience to an introverted meditation (is this, that he he has taken) a dangerous path, dangerous not because we fear we would discourage any exploration of the human spirit but because it so easily leads to futility."

Although Devree does, this (from Apollo,

77. In a note on Le Parfum de Combray by P. L. Larcher, the New Yorker, in one of its numbers for February, 1946,[1] said that it was at Combray that Marcel Proust, when young, was accustomed to visit his uncle Jules Amiot "summers" "until hay fever prevented his further collecting these[2] seasonal souvenirs, a precious if peculiar harvest which seems[3] only chaff to the young postwar French. These young Maquis intellectuals, disoriented and restless, spurn left-over literature as unreal."[4]

78. "Naturally,[5] Klee's anarchic ideals and anarchic personality appeal to *that*[6] of Herbert Read, whose great contribution to aesthetic thought has been the demand that an artist should have the right to find and pursue his own vision untrammelled by traditional art or cross reference to the appearances of nature. . [. .] Part of the . . [.] risk[7] taken by the extreme individualist in art: that he has deliberately departed from common experience to an introverted meditation[8] (is this, that [word][9] he has taken) a dangerous path,[10] dangerous not because in fear we would discourage any exploration of the human spirit but because it so easily leads to futility[.]"
    Although poorly done, this (from Apollo,

[1] Genêt [Janet Flanner], "Letter from Paris," *New Yorker*, 23 Feb. 1946, pp. 49-50.
[2] Source: those
[3] Source: if very peculiar harvest, which seem
[4] Source: leftover literature as being unreal.
[5] Source: begins indented paragraph
[6] Source: that
[7] Source: [. . .] That is part of the great risk
[8] Source: meditation.
[9] The doubtful word appears to be another *he*.
[10] Source: [. . .] But anarchy is a dangerous path,

Feb, 1946, p.283 in g value

Tous les hommes que l'on voit passer ont le même nombre exactement d'ancêtres. Mais leur immense majorité n'a légué, avec la flore multipliée de leurs instincts, que les séquelles de la servitude

　　　　　Labyrinthe (Genève), Juin, 1946

The only enjoyment of property that the destitute can enjoy is its destruction

　　　　　Stanley Morrison, The Typographic
　　　　　Arts in Edinburgh, 1944

In this book he speaks of "the permanent ap-
petite of mankind" for ornament in its tene-
ments, books &c

Lo característico del momento es que
el alma vulgar, sabiéndose vulgar, tiene
el denuedo de afirmar el derecho
de la vulgaridad y lo impone dondequiera.
　　　　　Ortega y Gasset

["easy"] comfort declares in The Song of Lazarus "
　　　　　　I have been raised again...
　　not by Christ but by Poetry "
　　　　　Life of Lucen. Jan 1947　p 62

Feb. 1946, p. 28[1]) is of value.

79. Tous[2] les hommes que l'on voit passer ont le même nombre exactement d'ancêtres. Mais leur immense majorité n'a legué,[3] avec la flore multipliée de leurs instincts, que les sequelles[4] de la servitude[.][5]
    Labyrinthe (Genève), Juin, 1946[6]

80. The only enjoyment of property that the destitute can enjoy is its destruction[.]
    Stanley Morrison, The Typographic Arts . . [. ,] Edinburgh, 1944[7]
    In this book he speaks of "the permanent[8] appetite of mankind" for ornament in its tenements, books etc

81. Lo caractéristico[9] del momento es que el alma vulgar, sabiéndose vulgar, tiene el denuedo de afirmar el derecho de la vulgaridad y lo impone dondequiera.
                    Ortega y Gasset[10]

82. ⟦Alex⟧ "Comfort declares in *The Song of Lazarus*,
            I have been raised again . . [.]
        not by Christ but by Poetry"[11]
        Life & Letters Jan 1947 p. 62[12]

[1] Perspex [pseud.], "Scylla and Charybdis," *Apollo*, 43 (Feb. 1946), 28.

[2] Source: begins indented paragraph

[3] Source: légué,

[4] Source: séquelles

[5] "All the men one sees passing by have exactly the same number of ancestors. But the vast majority of them have bequeathed, together with the multiplied flora of their instincts, only the consequences of servitude."

[6] Thadée Natanson, "Toulouse-Lautrec," *Labyrinthe*, No. 20 (June 1946), p. 3, col. 1.

[7] Stanley Morison [not Morrison], *The Typographic Arts: Past, Present and Future* (Edinburgh: James Thin, 1944), p. 10. In the next sentence, Stevens quotes from p. 41 of the book.

[8] Source: a permanent

[9] Sic, for característico

[10] This passage appears, italicized, in the next-to-last paragraph of Chapter One of Ortega's *La rebelión de las masas* (1930). In the anonymous "authorized" English translation, *The Revolt of the Masses*, 25th ed. (New York: Norton, 1957), the passage is rendered thus: "*The characteristic of the hour is that the commonplace mind, knowing itself to be commonplace, has the assurance to proclaim the rights of the commonplace and to impose them wherever it will*" (p. 18).
    In his correspondence with José Rodríguez Feo, Stevens mentions reading a number of Spanish-language periodicals, including *Sur* (Buenos Aires), *El Sol* (Madrid), and *Cuadernos Americanos* (Mexico); see *Secretaries of the Moon*, ed. Coyle and Filreis, pp. 34, 39, 91. It was possibly in one of these or even Rodríguez Feo's *Orígenes* that he found this quotation.

[11] Source: As Comfort declares in *The Song of Lazarus*:

        . . ."I have been raised again . . .
        not by Christ but by Poetry' . . .

[12] Neville Braybrooke, rev. of *The Triumph of Death*, by C. F. Ramuz, *Life and Letters and the London Mercury*, 52 (Jan. 1947), 62.

La nostalgie de l'éternel est au fond
de toutes les oeuvres des philosophes, des
romanciers et des poètes.

André Rousseaux

L'explication orphique de la Terre ... est le
seul devoir du poète.

Mallarmé

Le Moderne dédaigne d'imaginer.

Mallarmé   Divagations (177)

"Poetry is, of all others, the most daring form
of research"

Ponge and the Creative Method by Betty
Miller, Horizon, September 1947 p. 216

... Of all mental systems, the Freudian psychology
is the one which makes poetry indigenous to the
very constitution of the mind. Indeed, the mind,
as Freud sees it, is in the greater part of its
tendency, exactly a poetry-making organ. This
puts the case too strongly, no doubt, for it seems
to make the working of the unconscious mind
equivalent to poetry itself, forgetting that
between the unconscious mind and the
finished poem there supervene the social
interests and the formal control of the conscious

83. La nostalgie de l'eternel[1] est au fond de toutes les oeuvres des philosophes, des romanciers et des poetes.[2]
André Rousseaux[3]

84. L'explication orphique de la Terre . . [.] est le seul devoir du poète.[4]
Mallarmé[5]

85. Le Moderne dédaigne d'imaginer.[6]
Mallarmé   Divagations (137)[7]

86. "Poetry[8] is, of all others, the most daring form of research[.]"[9]
Ponge And The Creative Method by Betty Miller, Horizon, September
1947 p. 216[10]

87. [".] . . Of all[11] mental systems, the Freudian psychology is the one which
makes poetry indigenous to the very constitution of the mind. Indeed, the
mind, as Freud sees it, is in the greater part of its tendency, exactly a poetry-making organ. This puts the case too strongly, no doubt, for it seems
to make the working of the unconscious mind equivalent to poetry itself,
forgetting that between the unconscious mind and the finished poem
there supervene the social intention and the formal control of the conscious

[1] Source: La croyance à l'immortalité, ou à défaut la nostalgie de l'éternel,
[2] Source: poètes. "[The belief in immortality, or lacking that] the nostalgia for the eternal[,] is the basis of all the works of philosophers, novelists, and poets."
[3] Rev. of *Tous les hommes sont mortels*, by Simone de Beauvoir, *Le Littéraire* [weekly literary supplement of *Le Figaro*], 28 Dec. 1946, p. 2, col. 1.
[4] "The orphic explication of the earth . . . is the sole duty of the poet. . . ." Speaking of music critic Paul Rosenfeld in "The Shaper" (1948), Stevens says, "Perhaps there existed for him an ideal *Schöpfung*, a world composed of music, but which did not whirl round in music alone; or of painting, but which did not expand in color and form alone; or of poetry, but which did not limit itself to the *explication orphique* of the poet" (*OP* 262).
[5] Stevens quotes the first part of a sentence from Mallarmé's letter to Verlaine of 16 Nov. 1885. Though Stevens' source is unknown, the passage can be found in Mallarmé's *Correspondance*, ed. Henri Mondor and Lloyd James Austin (Paris: Gallimard, 1965), II, 301.
[6] Source: d'imaginer [. . .]. "Modern man does not deign to imagine. . . ."
[7] Stéphane Mallarmé, *Divagations* (Genève: Éditions d'Art Albert Skira, 1943), p. 137. This excerpt is from "Richard Wagner: Rêverie d'un poète français."
[8] Source: [. . .] poetry
[9] Compare Stevens' "Poetry is the scholar's art" (*OP* 167, *NA* 61).
[10] Betty Miller, "Francis Ponge and the Creative Method," *Horizon*, 16 (Sept. 1947), 216.
[11] Source: For, of all

minds. yet the statement has at least the virtue of counterbalancing the belief, so commonly expressed or implied, that the very opposite is true, and that poetry is a kind of beneficent aberration of the minds right course.

Freud has not merely naturalized poetry; he has discovered its status as a pioneer settler, and he sees it as a method of thought..

Freud showed, too, how the mind, in one of its parts, could work without logic, yet not without that driving purpose, that control of intent from which, perhaps it might be said, logic springs ... The unconscious mind in its struggle with the conscious always turns from the general to the concrete and finds the tangible trifle more congenial than the large abstraction."

      Freud And Literature By Lionel Trilling
      Horizon, September 1947 p 196/7

"Brisé en plein essor par l'effondrement de l'Empire, la jeunesse de 1820 à 1850 était impatiente de revivre, d'admirer, de tressaillir de nouveau: Scott était l'éveilleur d'enthousiasme que le monde attendait"

      P. Vervrier, Walter Scott,
       Tours 1935 pp 132-3 cited in
       French Studies I, 4, p 354.

mind. Yet the statement has at least the virtue of counterbalancing the belief, so commonly expressed or implied, that the very opposite is true, and that poetry is a kind of beneficent aberration of the mind's right course.

Freud[1] has not merely naturalized poetry; he has discovered its status as a pioneer settler, and he sees it as a method of thought. . [. .]

Freud[2] showed, too, how the mind, in one of its parts, could work without logic, yet not without that directing purpose, that control of intent from which, perhaps it might be said, logic springs. . [. .] The unconscious mind in its struggle with the conscious always turns from the general to the concrete and finds the tangible trifle more congenial than the large abstraction[.]"

Freud And Literature By Lionel Trilling Horizon, September 1947 p 196/7[3]

88. "Brisée en plein essor par l'effondrement de l'Empire, la jeunesse de 1820 à 1830 était impatiente de recréer, d'admirer, de tressaillir de nouveau: Scott était l'éveilleur d'enthousiasme que le monde attendait[.]"[4]

P. Genevrier, Walter Scott, Tours 1935 pp 132-3 cited in French Studies I, 4, p. 334.[5]

[1] Source: begins indented paragraph

[2] Source: begins indented paragraph

[3] Lionel Trilling, "Freud and Literature," *Horizon*, 16 (Sept. 1947), 196-97. If Stevens saw in Freud's *The Future of an Illusion* much that he considered hostile to poetry (*NA* 15), he also maintained in 1936 that Freud "has given the irrational a legitimacy that it never had before" (*OP* 219).

[4] "Broken in full flight by the collapse of the Empire, the young generation of 1820 to 1830 was impatient to rebuild, to admire, to be thrilled again: Scott was the awakener of enthusiasm whom society was awaiting."

[5] Genévrier (not Genevrier) is quoted in A. Lytton Sells, "Leconte de Lisle and Sir Walter Scott," *French Studies*, 1 (Oct. 1947), 334.

Un écrivain, à mon sens, a parfaitement le droit de se tromper... Après tout, ce n'est ni un prêtre, ni un mage. Il y a dans tout œuvre qui sort de ses mains une part de risque; et j'en vois plus d'un, parmi les meilleurs, qui travaille à la façon d'un artisan, construit par à-coups, se corrige sans cesse et grandit d'erreur en erreur.

Jean Paulhan. Lettre (de C.N.E.)

In a review of Middle Span by George Santayana, in The New Statesman & N. June 26, 1948, Raymond Mortimer joined him with Picasso as the two living Spaniards most conspicuous for genius and said

" they have both chosen to be expatriates yet retain under their cosmopolitanism a deep Spanishness — the sense "that in the service of love and imagination nothing can be too lavish, too sublime or too festive; yet that all this passion is a caprice, a farce, a contortion, a comedy of illusions "

Pascal. - Pensées. Chap. IV
Imagination. - C'est cette partie décevante dans l'homme, cette maîtresse d'erreur et de fausseté, et d'autant plus fourbe qu'elle ne l'est pas toujours; car elle serait règle infaillible de vérité, si elle l'était infaillible du mensonge. Mais étant

89. Un écrivain, à mon sens, a parfaitement le droit de se tromper. . [. .] Après tout, ce n'est ni un prêtre,[1] ni un mage. Il y a dans tout oeuvre[2] qui sort de ses mains une part de risque; et j'en vois plus d'un, parmi les meilleurs, qui travaille à la façon d'un artisan, construit par à-coups, se corrige sans cesse et grandit d'erreur en erreur.[3]

       Jean Paulhan, Lettre (de C. N. E.)[4]

90. In a review of *Middle Span* by George Santayana, in *The New Statesman etc* June 26, 1948,[5] Raymond Mortimer joined him with Picasso as the two living Spaniards most conspicuous for genius and said

      . . [.] they have both[6] chosen to be expatriates yet retain under their cosmopolitanism a deep Spanishness—the sense "that in the service of love and imagination nothing can be too lavish, too sublime[7] or too festive; yet that all this passion is a caprice, a farce, a contortion, a comedy of illusions''.[8]

91. Pascal.—Pensées. Chap. IV[9]

      Imagination.—C'est cette partie décevante[10] dans l'homme, cette maitresse[11] d'erreur et de fausseté, et d'autant plus fourbe qu'elle ne l'est pas toujours; car elle serait règle infaillible de vérité, si elle l'était infaillible du mensonge. Mais étant

---

[1] Sic, for prêtre,

[2] Sic, for toute oeuvre

[3] "A writer, in my opinion, has a perfect right to make mistakes. . . . After all, he is neither a priest nor a wizard. There is in every work that comes from his hands an element of risk; and I see more than one among the best who works in the manner of a craftsman, building by fits and starts, correcting himself ceaselessly and growing from error to error."

[4] During the German occupation of France, Paulhan was one of the more distinguished members of the Comité National des Écrivains (CNE), a resistance group that attacked collaborationist writers and periodicals in the pages of *Les Lettres Françaises*. After the liberation, however, Paulhan reacted against the CNE's blacklisting of collaborators. He resigned from the CNE and circulated a series of open letters in May-September 1947, arguing against an *épuration* of the kind then being conducted in the political and business spheres. Barbara Church sent copies of these letters to Stevens later that year. In his reply of 7 Jan. 1948, he says, "I have copied the last paragraph of the first page of the last letter into a book in which I collect things that I don't want to forget" (*L* 574). A slightly different version of the letter is reprinted in Paulhan's *Oeuvres complètes* (Paris: Cercle du Livre Précieux, 1970), V, 331-32. For a fuller account of Paulhan's dispute with the CNE, see Herbert R. Lottman, *The Purge* (New York: William Morrow, 1986), pp. 234-42.

[5] Raymond Mortimer, "A Philosophic Life," rev. of *The Middle Span*, by George Santayana, *New Statesman and Nation*, 26 June 1948, pp. 526-27; excerpt from p. 526.

[6] Source: both have

[7] Source: sublime,

[8] Mortimer quotes from p. 2 of *The Middle Span* (London: Constable, 1948), the second volume of *Persons and Places*. Stevens uses part of the quotation, without attributing it to Santayana, in "Imagination as Value" (1948, *NA* 154). Among his books at the Huntington Library are all three volumes of *Persons and Places*, published in New York by Charles Scribner's Sons.

le plus souvent fausse, elle ne donne aucune marque de sa qualité, marquant du même caractère le vrai et le faux.

Je ne parle pas des fous, je parle des plus sages; et c'est parmi eux que l'imagination a le grand don de persuader les hommes. La raison a beau crier, elle ne peut mettre le prix aux choses.

Cette superbe puissance, ennemie de la raison, qui se plaît à la contrôler et à la dominer, pour montrer combien elle peut en toutes choses, a établi dans l'homme une seconde nature. Elle a ses heureux, ses malheureux, ses sains, ses malades, ses riches, ses pauvres; elle fait croire, douter, nier la raison; elle suspend les sens, elle les fait sentir; elle a ses fous et ses sages; et rien ne nous dépite davantage que de voir qu'elle remplit ses hôtes d'une satisfaction bien autrement pleine et entière que la raison. Les habiles par imagination se plaisent tout autrement à eux-mêmes que les prudents ne se peuvent raisonnablement plaire. Ils regardent les gens avec empire; ils disputent avec hardiesse et confiance, les autres avec crainte et défiance; et cette gaieté de visage leur donne souvent l'avantage dans l'opinion des écoutants, tant les sages imaginaires ont de faveur auprès des juges de même nature. Elle ne peut rendre sages les fous; mais elle les rend heureux, à l'envi de la raison, qui ne peut rendre ses amis que misérables, l'une les couvrant de gloire, l'autre de honte.

le plus souvent fausse, elle ne donne aucune marque de sa qualité, marquant de même caractère le vrai et le faux.

Je ne parle pas des fous, je parle des plus sages; et c'est parmi eux que l'imagination a le grand don de persuader les hommes. La raison a beau crier, elle ne peut mettre le prix aux choses.[1]

Cette superbe puissance, ennemie de la raison, qui se plait[2] à la contrôler et à la dominer, pour montrer combien elle peut en toutes choses, a établi dans l'homme une seconde nature. Elle a ses heureux, ses malheureux, ses sains, ses malades, ses riches, ses pauvres; elle fait croire, douter, nier la raison; elle suspend les sens, elle les fait sentir; elle a ses fous et ses sages; et rien ne nous dépite davantage que de voir qu'elle remplit ses hôtes d'une satisfaction bien autrement pleine et entière que la raison. Les habiles par imagination se plaisent tout autrement à eux-mêmes que les prudents ne se peuvent raisonnablement plaire. Ils regardent les gens avec empire; ils disputent avec hardiesse et confiance; les autres avec crainte et défiance; et cette gaieté de visage leur donne souvent l'avantage dans l'opinion des écoutants, tant les sages imaginaires ont de faveur auprès des juges de même nature. Elle ne peut rendre sages les foux;[3] mais elle les rend heureux, à l'envi de la raison, qui ne peut rendre ses amis que miserables,[4] l'une les couvrant de gloire, l'autre de honte.

---

[9] In his *Pascal's* Pensées, *with an English Translation, Brief Notes and Introduction* (New York: Pantheon, 1950), H. F. Stewart preserves Pascal's old-fashioned spelling but otherwise offers a version of the French text that corresponds closely to the unidentified text quoted by Stevens; in subsequent notes, I call attention to the more significant departures from Stewart's text. For Stewart's translation of these excerpts, see the Appendix, pp. 111-12.

[10] Stewart: dominante ["ruling"]

[11] Sic, for maîtresse

---

[1] Stevens has drawn a small arrow in the left margin, pointing to this sentence.

[2] Sic, for se plaît

[3] Stewart: rendre les sages fous;

[4] Sic, for misérables,

Qui dispense la réputation? qui donne le respect et la vénération aux personnes, aux ouvrages, aux lois, aux grands, sinon cette faculté imaginante? Toutes les richesses de la terre sont insuffisantes sans son consentement....

Nos magistrats ont bien connu ce mystère. Leurs robes rouges, leurs hermines dont ils s'emmaillottent en chats fourrés, les palais où ils jugent, les fleurs de lis, tout cet appareil auguste était fort nécessaire; et si les médecins n'avaient des soutanes et des mules, et que les docteurs n'eussent des bonnets carrés et des robes trop amples de quatre parties, jamais ils n'auraient dupé le monde qui ne peut résister à cette montre si authentique. Les seuls gens de guerre ne se sont pas déguisés de la sorte, parce qu'en effet leur part est plus essentielle: ils s'établissent par la force, les autres par grimace.

C'est ainsi que nos rois n'ont pas recherché ces déguisements. Ils ne se sont pas masqués d'habits extraordinaires pour paraître tels; mais ils se sont accompagnés de gardes, de hallebardes; ces troupes armées qui n'ont de mains et de force que pour eux, les trompettes et les tambours qui marchent audevant, et ces légions qui les environnent, font trembler les plus fermes. Ils n'ont pas l'habit seulement, ils ont la force. Il faudrait avoir une raison bien épurée pour regarder comme un autre homme le Grand Seigneur environné,

Qui dispense la reputation?[1] qui donne le respect et la vénération aux personnes, aux ouvrages, aux lois, aux grands, sinon cette faculté imaginante? Toutes les richesses de la terre sont insuffisantes sans son consentement. . . [.]

Nos magistrats ont bien connu ce mystère. Leurs robes rouges, leurs hermines dont ils s'emmaillotent en chats fourrés, les palais où ils jugent, les fleur[2] de lis, tout cet appareil auguste était fort nécessaire; et si les médecins n'avaient des soutanes et des mules, et que les docteurs n'eussent des bonnets carrés et des robes trop amples de quatre parties, jamais ils n'auraient dupé le monde qui ne peut résister[3] à cette montre si authentique. Les seuls[4] gens de guerre ne se sont past déguisés de la sorte, parce qu'en effet leur part est plus essentielle: ils s'établissent par la force, les autres par grimace.

C'est ainsi que nos rois n'ont pas recherché ces déguisements. Ils ne se sont pas masqués d'habits extraordinaires pour paraître tels; mais ils se sont accompagnés de gardes, de hallebardes: ces trognes armées qui n'ont de mains et de force que pour eux, les trompettes et les tambours qui marchent audevant,[5] et ces légions qui les environnent, font trembler les plus fermes. Ils n'ont pas l'habit seulement, ils ont la force. Il faudrait avoir une raison bien épurée pour regarder comme un autre homme le Grand Seigneur environné,

[1] Sic, for réputation?
[2] Sic, for fleurs
[3] Stewart: qui ne résiste
[4] Stewart: authentique. [. . .] Les seuls
[5] Sic, for au-devant,

dans son superbe sérail, de quarante mille janissaires
... L'imagination dispose de tout; elle fait la beauté,
la justice et le bonheur, qui est le tout du monde.
Je voudrais de bon cœur voir le livre italien, dont
je ne connais que le titre, qui vaut lui seul bien des
livres: Della opinione regina del mondo

Pascal. – Pensées. Chap. IX, XXXI Beauté poétique.
... Mais qui s'imaginera une femme sur
ce modèle-là qui consiste à dire de petites choses
avec de grands mots, verra une jolie demoiselle toute
pleine de miroirs et de chaînes, dont il rira,
parce qu'on sait mieux en quoi consiste l'agrément
d'une femme que l'agrément des vers.

The New Statesman – July 31, 1948 p. 91, Logical
Positivism, Fascism And Value, C.E.M. Joad
        The traditional philosophy of Western Europe
holds that transcending the familiar world of things
known to us by our senses and explored by science,
there is another order of reality which contains
values. Of these, Goodness, Beauty, and Truth are
preeminent and are the source of ethics, aesthetics
and logic respectively. In other words, it is because
the universe is, or contains, a moral order that
somethings are right and some wrong, because it
contains an aesthetic order that some things
are beautiful and some ugly, and because

dans son superbe sérail, de quarante mille janissaires. . [. .] L'imagination dispose de tout; elle fait la beauté, la justice et le bonheur, qui est le tout du monde. Je voudrais de bonne coeur voir le livre italien, dont je ne connais que le titre, qui vaut lui[1] seul bien des livres: Della opinione regina del mondo[.]

Pascal.—Pensées. Chap. IX, XXVI *Beauté poetique.*[2]
  . . [.] Mais qui s'imaginera une femme sur ce modèle-lá[3] qui consiste à dire de petites choses avec de grand[4] mots, verra une jolie demoiselle toute pleine de miroirs et de chaines,[5] dont il rira, parce qu'on sait mieux en quoi consiste l'agrément d'une femme que l'agrément des vers.[6]

92. The New Statesman . . [. ,] July 31, 1948 p. 91, Logical Positivism, Facism[7] And Value, C. E. M. Joad[8]
  The traditional philosophy of Western Europe holds that[9] transcending the familiar world of things known to us by our senses and explored by science, there is another order of reality which contains values. Of these, Goodness, Beauty and Truth are preëminent[10] and are the source of ethics, aesthetics and logic respectively. In other words, it is because the universe is, or contains, a moral order that somethings[11] are right and some wrong; because it contains an aesthetic order that some things are beautiful and some ugly, and because

[1] Stewart: vaut à luy
[2] Sic, for *poétique.*
[3] Sic, for modèle-là
[4] Sic, for grands
[5] Sic, for chaînes,
[6] Stevens paraphrases and discusses the excerpt on imagination in his lecture "Imagination as Value" (1948, *NA* 133-36). The epigraph to his early poem "Phases" (1914, *OP* 3) is also from the *Pensées* (pp. 220-21 in Stewart).
[7] Sic, for Fascism
[8] C. E. M. Joad, "Logical Positivism, Fascism and Value," *New Statesman and Nation*, 31 July 1948, p. 91.
[9] Source: that,
[10] Source: pre-eminent,
[11] Source: some things

there is such a thing as truth that some judgments are true and some false. Many philosophers would also add that the universe also includes deity, who is the source of the values, Goodness, Truth and Beauty, being, as religion puts it, the modes of God's revelation of Himself to man. Metaphysics — the study of the reality which transcends and underlies the familiar world — is, therefore, in part, the study of the values and of God. . .

Philosophy, as traditionally conceived, may be described as a sustained endeavour to understand the universe as a whole. . . Philosophy has, therefore, had the dual purpose of revealing truth and increasing virtue. . . If Professor Ayer is right, this endeavour is mistaken, precisely because there is no such thing as value.

Pour être mort, malheureusement il faut mourir.
        Quoted by Dean Inge. Philosophy, Nov. 1946 p.201

The verse of Matthew Arnold "contains no sudden tremendous glimpses into the life of man and nature.. His vividness is the vividness of prose. The nice price of observation.. does not produce that sense of imaginative illumination which is one of the chiefest gifts of poetry"
        Peter Quennell, New Statesman, Nov. 6, 1948. 399

there is such a thing as truth that some judgments are true and some false. Many philosophers would also add[1] that the universe also includes deity, who[2] is the source of the values, Goodness, Truth and Beauty, being, as religion puts it, the modes of God's revelation of Himself to man. Metaphysics—the study of the reality which transcends and underlies the familiar world—is, therefore, in part, the study of the values and of God. . . [.]

Philosophy, as traditionally conceived, may be described as a sustained endeavour to understand the universe as a whole. . [. .] Philosophy has, therefore, had the dual purpose of revealing truth and increasing virtue. . [. .] If Professor Ayer is right, this endeavour is mistaken, precisely because there is no such thing as value.[3]

93. Pour être mort, malheureusement il faut mourir.[4]
    Quoted by Dean Inge, Philosophy, Nov. 1946 p. 201[5]

94. The verse of Matthew Arnold "contains no sudden tremendous glimpses into the life of man and nature. . [. .] His vividness is the vividness of prose. The nice piece of observation . . [.] does not produce that sense of imaginative illumination which is one of the chiefest gifts of poetry[.]"
    Peter Quennell, New Statesman, Nov. 6, 1948, 399[6]

---

[1] Source: would add

[2] Source: deity who

[3] Stevens quotes from p. 91 of this review in "Imagination as Value" (1948, *NA* 138), as well as from Ayer's *Language, Truth and Logic* (*NA* 137).

[4] "To be dead, unfortunately, one must die."

[5] W. R. Inge, "The Philosophy of Berdyaeff," *Philosophy*, 21 (Nov. 1946), 201. Stevens transcribed another passage from the same page of Inge's essay onto the front flyleaf of his copy of Nicolas Berdyaev's (or Berdyaeff's) *Solitude and Society*, trans. George Reavey (London: Geoffrey Bles, Centenary Press, 1938). This book is at the University of Massachusetts Library.

[6] Peter Quennell, rev. of *Matthew Arnold: An Introduction and a Selection*, by Clifford Dyment, *New Statesman and Nation*, 6 Nov. 1948, p. 399.

... problèmes des dimanches .. Comment toucher
le grand public .. La redoutable problème littéraire
de la vulgarisation.

Of Pascal, French Studies, Oct. 1948

"The descriptions, on page after page, have the cohesiveness,
the fusion of words into a new whole that we associate with genuine poetry."

Fr. a review in Life and Letters, Sept. 1949, p. 259.

"The later proliferations of romantic and symbolist theory, have tended to obscure one of the
most valuable functions of poetry: the illumination of the usual."

Edward Sackville. West: Goethe in
New Statesman & Nation, Oct 8, 1949, p. 387

And in comedy, as in other forms of
poetry, suggestion is enough.

From Molière, A New Criticism.
By W. G. Moore. Oxford: Clarendon Press.

For (Fondane) true poetry has no relation with
the Idea, it springs from the gouffre, from
the hidden, primitive sources of life, rebellious
to the formal constructions, ideological
or technical, of men. And certain artists
are aware of this, if only dimly, half-

95. sa plume[1] des dimanches . . [.] Comment toucher le grand public[2]. . [.] la redoutable problème[3] littéraire de la vulgarization.[4]
    Of Pascal, French Studies, Oct. 1948[5]

96. "The descriptions, on page after page, have the cohesiveness, the fusion of words into a new whole that we associate with genuine poetry."[6]
    Fr. a review in Life And Letters, Sept. 1949, p. 259.[7]

97. "the later[8] proliferations of romantic and symbolist theory have tended to obscure one of the most valuable functions of poetry: the illumination of the usual."
    Edward Sackville-West: Goethe in New Statesman & Nation, Oct 8, 1949, p. 387[9]

98. And in comedy, as in other forms of poetry, suggestion is enough.
    From Molière: A New Criticism.
    By W. G. Moore. Oxford: Clarendon Pr.[10]

99. For (Fondane)[11] true poetry has no relation with the Idea, it springs from the *gouffre*,[12] from the hidden, primitive sources of life, rebellious to the formal constructions, ideological or technical, of men. And certain artists are aware of this, if only dimly, half-

---

[1] Source: Mais chaque fois qu'il prend sa plume

[2] Source: public?

[3] Sic, for le redoutable problème
Source: Descartes, en un mot, faisait face—et l'un des premiers—au redoutable problème

[4] Source: vulgarisation. "[But each time he takes up] his Sunday quill . . . How to affect the general public? . . . [Descartes, in a word, was facing—and as one of the first—] the daunting literary problem of vulgarization." Stevens concludes his 1 Dec. 1948 letter to José Rodríguez Feo with the sentence, "Let me have a few zips from your plume de Dimanche now and then" (*L* 625).

[5] Gilbert Gadoffre, "Le *Discours de la Méthode* et l'histoire littéraire," *French Studies*, 2 (Oct. 1948), 310-11. Stevens mentions this issue of *French Studies* in his letter to Rodríguez Feo (*L* 624). The passage from which these excerpts are taken deals not with Pascal but with Descartes and what he learned from Balzac.

[6] Source: poetry [. . .].

[7] Bernard Wall, rev. of *Conversation in Sicily*, by Elio Vittorini, trans. Wilfred David, *Life and Letters and the London Mercury*, 62 (Sept. 1949), 259.

[8] Source: At the same time it must be admitted that the later

[9] Edward Sackville West, "Goethe in 1949," *New Statesman and Nation*, 8 Oct. 1949, p. 387.

[10] Will Grayburn Moore, *Molière: A New Criticism* (Oxford: Clarendon Press, 1949), p. 117.

[11] Source: For him

[12] "*abyss*"

consciously and reluctantly. Baudelaire is one
of these artists and the basic message of his poetry
is this sense of the gouffre .. Even Baudelaire, while
urging that 'la grande poésie est bête : elle croit',
gives frequent colours to the traditional view that
art is 'un reflet de l'idée'. Himself horrified
by the elements thrown up by the gouffre, 'il a
recours entre eux aux exorcismes, aux incantations de l'Idée qu'il apprend par cœur et répète
comme un perroquet savant.' Baudelaire's
objection is not to external bonds but to internal
(the ideals of mesure, prudence, obéissance, sérénité): he feels instinctively that a revolution
in the matter of the poem requires banality of
form.

> French Studies, January 1950 pp. 60-61
> in a review of Baudelaire et l'expérience
> du gouffre, by Benj. Fondane, by
> C. T. Clapton

Un écrivain authentique explore un univers authentique, sous la conduite d'une nécessité
intérieure. Et cela compte seul.

> Jacques Tournier, La Table Ronde, mars 1950, p. 159

It needs the supernatural to make the tedium
of the natural world tolerable.

> Nicholas Davenport on Country Magic in

consciously and reluctantly. Baudelaire is one of these artists and the basic message of his poetry is this sense of the gouffre.[1] . [. .] Even Baudelaire, while urging that 'la grande poésie est bête: elle croit',[2] gives frequent colour to the traditional view that art is 'un reflet de l'idée'.[3] Himself horrified by the elements thrown up by the gouffre,[4] 'il a recours contre eux aux exorcismes, aux incantations de l'Idée qu'il apprend par coeur et répète comme un perroquet savant.'[5] Baudelaire's objection is not to external bonds but to internal (the ideals of mesure, prudence, obéissance, sérénité[6]): he feels[7] instinctively that a revolution in the matter of the poem requires banalité[8] of form.

French Studies, January 1950 pp. 60-61 in a review of Baudelaire et l'expérience du gouffre, by Benj. Fondane, by G. T. Clapton[9]

100. Un écrivain authentique explore un univers authentique, sous la conduite d'une nécessité intérieure. Et cela compte seul.[10]

Jacques Tournier, La Table Rond, Mars 1950, p. 159[11]

101. It needs the supernatural to make the tedium of the natural world tolerable.

Nicholas Davenport on Country Magic in

[1] Source: *gouffre.*
[2] "great poetry is stupid: it believes"
[3] "a reflection of the idea"
[4] Source: *gouffre,*
[5] Source: savant'. "[H]e has recourse against them to exorcisms, to incantations of the Idea which he knows by heart and repeats like an erudite parrot."
[6] Source: mesure . . . sérénité ("proportion, prudence, obedience, serenity") italicized
[7] Source: he even feels
[8] Source: *banalité*
[9] G. T. Clapton, rev. of *Baudelaire et l'expérience du gouffre*, by Benjamin Fondane, *French Studies*, 4 (Jan. 1950), 60-61.
[10] "An authentic writer explores an authentic universe, under the guidance of an inner necessity. And that is all that counts."
[11] Jacques Tournier, "Poètes romanciers," *La Table Ronde* [not *Rond*], Mar. 1950, p. 159.

The New Statesman, June 3, 1950.
(Poetry as Supernaturalism)

The value of poetry .. and the term includes
religion and philosophy .. is that it devotes
itself to the business of transmuting incoherence
into romance

　　　Santayana's Literary Psychology, Chas.
T. Harrison, Sewanee Review, Spring 1953, p.218

Par pente intime, amour des belles ordonnances, il a surtout usé des formes
poétiques éprouvées. mais il n'y a rien en
lui du ronronnant faiseur d'alexandrins.
　　　Émile Henriot par Henri Perruchot
　　　Revue de la Pensée Française, Avril
　　　1953, p. 11

Tal-Coat
　　　　　Revenu à Paris .. il semble s'isoler dans
une esthétique extrêmement austère

　　　　　On peut se demander comment il sortira
de cette voie, s'il adoptera et inventera un nouveau
réalisme, ou si, au contraire, il obéira aux appels
de l'abstraction. Ce sera bien étonnant et bien con-
tradictoire avec ce qu'on sait de lui. Plus vraisemblablement on peut espérer pour les prochaines et
après, cette synthèse que tout le monde attend

[1950-1953?]

The New Statesman, June 3, 1950.[1]
(Poetry as Supernaturalism)

102. The value of poetry . . [.] and the term includes religion and philosophy
. . [.] is[2] that it devotes itself to the business of transmuting incoherence
into romance[.]

Santayana's Literary Psychology, Chas. T. Harrison, Sewanee Review,
Spring 1953, p. 218[3]

103. Par pente intime, amour des belles ordonnances, il a surtout usé des
formes poétiques éprouvées, mais il n'y a rien en lui du ronronnant
faiseur d'alexandrins.[4]

Émile Henriot par Henri Perruchot Rev. de la Pensée Francaise, Avril
1953, p. 11[5]

104. *Tal-Coat*[6]

Revenu à Paris . . [.] il semble s'isoler dans une esthétique extrêmement austère[7]

On peut se demander comment il sortira de cette voie, s'il adoptera et
inventera un nouveau réalisme, ou si, au contraire, il obéira aux appels
de l'abstraction. Ce sera[8] bien étonnant et bien contradiction[9] avec ce
qu'on sait de lui. Plus vraisemblablement on peut espérer[10] pour les prochaines et apres,[11] cette synthèse que tout le monde attend

---

[1] Nicholas Davenport, "Country Magic," *New Statesman and Nation*, 3 June 1950, p. 629.

[2] Source: poetry, then—and the term includes religion and philosophy—is

[3] Charles T. Harrison, "Santayana's 'Literary Psychology,'" *Sewanee Review*, 61 (Spring 1953),
218.

[4] "From natural inclination, love of beautiful structures, he chiefly made use of established poetic forms, but there is nothing in him of the purring maker of alexandrines."

[5] Henri Perruchot, "Émile Henriot, ou la poésie de l'honnête homme," *Revue de la Pensée
Française*, 12 (Apr. 1953), 11.

[6] This passage is excerpted from Raymond Cogniat, "Tal-Coat," *Le Point*, No. 36 (Dec. 1947), p.
24. Stevens refers to this essay in letters to Paule Vidal of 6 Apr. and 4 May 1948 (*L* 583-84, 594-
95). The following year, he purchased the Tal-Coat still life that inspired his poem "Angel Sur-
rounded by Paysans" (1950, *CP* 496-97).

[7] Source: austère [. . .].

[8] Source: serait

[9] Source: bien en contradiction

[10] Source: espérer,

[11] Source: prochaines étapes,

et que personne n'a encore pu réaliser. Tal-Coat
est un des rares artistes que nous croyons capable
de cette création, indispensable si l'on veut voir
cesser dans l'art contemporain, un état d'incertitude où les absolus s'affrontent dangereusement et
s'isolent les uns les autres

et que personne n'a encore pu réaliser. Tal-Coat est un des rares artistes que nous croyions capables de cette création, indispensable si l'on veut voir cesser dans l'art contemporain, un état d'incertitude où les absolus s'affront[1] dangereusement et s'isolent les uns des autres[.][2]

---

[1] Source: s'affrontent

[2] "Back in Paris . . . he seems to isolate himself in an extremely austere aesthetic. . . .

We can wonder how he will emerge from this path, if he will take up and invent a new realism, or if, on the contrary, he will heed the appeal of abstraction. It should be very surprising and entirely at odds with what is known of him. More likely we can expect, during the coming stages, that synthesis which everyone awaits and which no one has yet been able to realize. Tal-Coat is one of the rare artists whom we have believed capable of this creation, indispensable if one wants to see the end in contemporary art of a state of uncertainty in which absolutes dangerously confront each other and are isolated from one another."

Appendix

Translation of the excerpts from Pascal's *Pensées* in Entry 91:

Imagination

I<small>T IS MAN'S</small> [DECEPTIVE] FACULTY, queen of lies and error, and all the greater deceiver for that she does not always deceive; for she would be an infallible touchstone of truth if she were a touchstone of falsehood. But being most often false she leaves no sure mark of her quality, for she sets the same stamp upon truth and falsehood.

I speak not of fools, but of the wisest of mankind among whom imagination exhibits her greatest power of persuasion. Reason protests to no purpose, she is incompetent to appraise things.

This haughty power, which loves to rule and lord it over reason, her foe, has bestowed upon man a second nature, just to show her great might. She has her fortunate followers and her unfortunate, her sound and sick, her rich, her poor; she causes Reason to believe, to doubt, to deny; she dulls the senses or sharpens them; she has her fools and her sages, and nothing vexes us more than to see her fill her minions with a satisfaction greater and more complete than Reason does. Men whose cleverness lies in their own imagination are far better pleased with themselves than sensible men can ever reasonably be. They look down arrogantly upon others; they argue with boldness and assurance; the sensible do so with timidity and mistrust; the sprightly air of those who imagine themselves wise often gives them an advantage in the minds of their hearers, such favour do they find with like-minded judges. Imagination cannot make fools wise, but she makes them happy, whereas Reason can only make her friends wretched; the former covers them with glory, the latter covers them with shame.

Who hands out reputations? Who apportions respect and veneration to people, to achievements, to laws, to the great, if not this faculty of imagination? All the wealth of the world would be insufficient without its help. . . .

Our magistrates know this secret. Their red robes, the ermine in which they wrap themselves like furry cats, the courts where they sit, the *fleurs-de-lis*—they needed all that solemn paraphernalia; and physicians without their cassocks and mules, and lawyers without their square caps and gowns four times too big, would never have taken in the world, which cannot resist so convincing a display. . . . Soldiers alone do not dress up like that, because the part they play is more substantial; they establish themselves by force, not by make-believe.

This is why our Kings have not resorted to such disguise. They do not don fancy dress in order to appear royal; they have the accompaniment of guards and pikes. The red-faced rogues whose hands and strength are dedicated to their protection, the drums and trumpets which go before them, and the legions which stand around them, make the stoutest hearts shake with fear.

They have more than the tunic, they have power. Only a very dry Reason can regard as a common man the Grand Turk in his proud seraglio with forty thousand janissaries about him. . . .

Imagination governs all; she creates beauty, justice, and happiness which are mankind's whole aim. I should much like to see the Italian book *Della opinione regina del mondo* of which I know but the title, but a title worth a whole library. . . .

Poetic Beauty

. . . But if you picture a woman in this way, that is by using big words to describe little things, you will behold a pretty girl smothered in looking-glasses and chains. This will move you to laughter, for you understand the nature of a woman's charm better than you do that of verse.

—H. F. Stewart, *Pascal's* Pensées, *with an English Translation, Brief Notes and Introduction* (New York: Pantheon, 1950), pp. 39-43, 503.

INDEX

Library of Congress Cataloging-in-Publication Data

Stevens, Wallace, 1879–1955.
  Sur plusieurs beaux sujects.

  Includes index.
  1. Commonplace-books.   I. Bates, Milton J.
II. Henry E. Huntington Library and Art Gallery.
III. Title.
PS3537.T4753S8   1989   818'.5203   88-61760
ISBN 0-8047-1549-1 (alk. paper)